ADVENTURER FLOYD GIBBONS:

EYE STREET'S EYEWITNESS TO HISTORY

To Bruce + Kate —

May you be as adventurous as floyd.

ADVENTURER FLOYD GIBBONS:

EYE STREET'S EYEWITNESS TO HISTORY

Paul Warren '68

By Paul Warren

All income from sales goes to a Gonzaga College High School scholarship. All costs and labor donated by Warren Communications News.

ISBN 978-1535418188

Contact author at pwarren@warren-news.com
Purchase book at floydgibbons.com

Warren Communications News
2115 Ward Ct. NW
Washington, D.C. 20037

To my wife and daughters, Katherine Norton Warren, Marie Warren O'Hara and Lucy Warren Bennett, for teaching me so much.

Contents

Preface

FLOYD GIBBONS, ADVENTURER, reads his tombstone. He was other things, but at his core, adventurer is what he was. Rarely had this country seen such a man and certainly we will not see another. A product of the late 19th and early 20th century, Gibbons rose to fame when it was still possible for someone to explore unexplored places, experience seemingly-impossible experiences and meet with then-approachable historical figures.

But to do these things, a man must be less afraid than anyone else. For whatever reason, Gibbons was. His choice of a career as a newspaperman and then broadcaster allowed him to try any dangerous stunt that came to mind, just to tell his readers and listeners what it felt like. And instead of terror, he often felt joy. From riding in a frightening auto race to facing German machine guns to trekking across the Sahara, Gibbons seemed to never falter in his optimism that he would not be hurt and still feel the thrill of whatever he was attempting.

It was this relentless optimism that was so American and so appealing to those in the United States after the pain of World War I and the deprivation of the stock market crash and ensuing Depression in the 1930s.

To follow Gibbons' path through the first half of the 20th century is to take a survey course in its history. Like a Forrest Gump with intellect and charm, Gibbons seemed to rub elbows with anyone of note from that period or be there when warfare erupted. His radio shows *The Headline Hunter* and *Adventurers' Club* summed up his raisons d'etre.

The world into which Gibbons was born in 1887 was one still guided by the Horatio Alger stories of boys of humble origins gaining fame and fortune through luck and pluck. Gibbons took them to heart, though without the wealthy patron who often helped the Alger characters. Instead, Gibbons continually reinvented himself in the American way, from newspaperman to book author to broadcaster to entrepreneur, toggling back and forth as needed. Previously, men like Davy Crockett, Buffalo Bill Cody and Teddy Roosevelt traveled similar paths.

Since the Gibbons days, technologies have made places far easier to reach and report from far more safely. The same technologies and medical advances that resulted in far fewer deaths for American troops in recent wars have made those wars safer for reporters to be embedded. A drone could have told the Marines a hidden machine gun lay in wait at a wheat field at Belleau Wood in 1918. Gibbons charged over the top there, resulting in three wounds and the loss of an eye. Getting hospital care took hours and one doctor erroneously thought his wounds fatal. In another instance, to document the millions starving in Russia in 1921, Gibbons had to expose himself to the very diseases that were decimating the Russians. A three-month trek across the Sahara in 1923 included few medicines, hostile tribes and even slavers. There was little or no communication with the outside world or means for an airlift to safety.

The word "adventurer" itself is becoming archaic. TV personalities showing us their adventures in the wild often have extensive resources at hand. American news media are as cautious as Gibbons' colleagues were in his day, which is what made him a unique adventurer then and now. *National Geographic* in 2014 published its list of Adventurers of the Year. Instead of Gibbons-like characters, runners, skiers, surfers, climbers and swimmers dominate the list.

The day of the adventurer has passed. This book is to keep the memory of one of those alive.

Fortunate Son

Foreword by Michael Dolan

Much of America and the world understands Washington, D.C.—wrongly—as a Plato's cave of shadowy conspiracy and blatant hegemony-mongering, through which cautious bureaucrats creep out their lives of quiet desperation.

Nonsense. Washington is and always has been a boom town, a lodestar for young people bent on making a mark. What are the House and Senate but carousels on which to reach for a succession of brass rings leading to the biggest and brassiest ring of all—the one that hangs at 1600 Pennsylvania Avenue NW?

The capital also functions as a powerful magnet, trapping in Spring Valley and Chevy Chase and along Connecticut Avenue's cave-dwelling canyons people of a certain age who, having long ago made their mark, long since should have surrendered to senescence and returned to the hinterlands that spawned them.

Between these poles flutters the Washington-of-the-mind that fascinates and disgusts so many onlookers who experience the city only at a distance.

D.C. natives know a different city, but still a boom town, and one that, as every boom town does, spawns ambitious children of its own. Growing up amid power and fame, some of Washington's offspring, intuiting how hard it is to become a hometown hero, light out for the territories in search of employment and adventure, preferably in the same package.

That's what Floyd Gibbons did, and what an arc he lit with his hunger to rip across the country and the world, across continents and eras, gulping experience as if famished and remanufacturing it into stories that gripped a generation. In print, on the radio and on the silver screen, Floyd Gibbons essentially invented the role of iconographic world-wandering reporter, the trouble man who can't stay away from danger because he wants to tell you how it felt when the speedometer went to three digits, when the flames ate through the beams, when the bullets and the bombs hit. His ambition was his gift, and in this book Paul Warren, another son of Washington, D.C., illuminates the extraordinary life of a hungry man who wanted so badly to be noticed, yet now is hardly known at all.

Michael Dolan is the editor of American History *magazine and the author of the book* The American Porch *and the play* Desert One.

Acknowledgments

If this book achieves the goal of telling us of the life of Adventurer Floyd Gibbons, there is one person I must first thank profusely for his help—Mike Dolan, editor of *American History* magazine. My friend since our days at Gonzaga College High School in Washington, D.C., Mike once again proved himself as the best book editor an author could seek. Time and time again he told me to fill holes in the story, add details and flesh out bare bones.

His curiosity made me find the names of Italian generals at war in Ethiopia or specifics on a German machine gun. His demands sometimes left me exasperated but I knew where his heart was. It was in the same place when he edited my last book, *In the Web of History: Gonzaga College and the Lincoln Assassination*, and when we co-edited *Echo Ever Proudly: Gonzaga College in the Press 1821-1899*.

His heart is at Gonzaga and with its alumni. Our books and a generous donation have yielded $144,654 for the Michael Kelly Scholarship Fund, which has given out $36,198 in financial aid to Gonzaga students. *Atlantic Magazine* Chairman David Bradley donated $50,000 to honor Kelly, the Gonzaga graduate who died in 2003 in Iraq while covering the war for the magazine.

Let me also thank my wife, Katherine Norton Warren, copy editor and cheerleader; my brother, Dan, and my sons, Christopher and Timothy, all of whom make their livings with words and improved mine immeasurably. Tim had the added wisdom to marry Anne Addison Warren, whose keen eye has also improved this book. Also, let me thank my brother-in-law Sean Maloney, a retired college librarian, for bringing an academic view to my manuscript. Thanks, too, to Hank Wieland for donating his meticulous proofreading services.

Key to my research was my sister Ellen Warren, a former *Chicago Daily News* foreign correspondent now with the *Chicago Tribune*, who helped steer me down Gibbons' adventurous path. She and Gibbons are neighbors in the Chicago Journalism Hall of Fame.

Thanks also to the staff at the Fogler Library at the University of Maine, Orono, for hefting up box upon box of the Floyd Gibbons collection from storage, and happily copying what I needed. Thanks to the staffs of the Newseum, the Marine Corps Museum in Quantico, Va., and Patty Stone for letting me into the archives of Gonzaga College High School. Thanks also to Georgetown University for digging up Gibbons' student alumni record.

Finally, a boisterous shout out to Greg Jones of Warren Communications News, who has completed 18 Marine Corps Marathons and just as determinedly helped prepare this and my previous book for publication. His work and advice has spared me a lot of tears over the mousepad.

Introduction

Floyd Gibbons sat in a lifeboat on the darkened sea. The boat could hold some 23 passengers and 23 were aboard. Hours ago their ship, *RMS Laconia*, had vanished in a hiss of steam as its boilers met the north Atlantic. Night enveloped the small craft, whose passengers could only pray that before the *Laconia* went down someone had sent a distress signal. It was February 25, 1917.

Unlike his companions, Gibbons was exactly where he wanted to be. A foreign correspondent for the *Chicago Tribune*, he had booked passage on the Cunard liner specifically because he had calculated that the *Laconia* had a good chance of being attacked by one of Germany's U-boats. If his wager paid off, he'd have the story of a lifetime—or a spectacular obituary. Gibbons gladly took the risk.

At 10:30 p.m. that winter Sunday, Gibbons, 29, had been in the smoking room at the stern discussing that very calculation when the *Laconia* shook slightly and a mild noise resonated through the ship. Gibbons later said the blow's meekness disappointed him. Meek or not, the German torpedo did fatal damage. Whistles blew and passengers and crew ran for the lifeboats. Lowered unevenly, the craft Gibbons had hopped into jerked and tilted. The stern was down, the bow was up and those aboard found themselves staring into black waters and grabbing at anything to keep from pitching into them. The lifeboat descended tortuously to the surface, where its panicked occupants hacked away the lines tethering them to the doomed *Laconia.*

There were eight oars. Led by an aged sailor, the passengers rowed feverishly. Once the frigid sea water reached the boilers, it would shatter them into shrapnel. And the sinking ship would suck down anything nearby. As Gibbons' lifeboat started to pull away, a figure splashed alongside the boat. The man had gotten tangled in the lines before he could jump clear and was pulled aboard the craft shivering. As the lifeboat slowly separated from the *Laconia* sad reality began to settle in.

"We prepared for the siege of the elements," Gibbons wrote later. "The black rim of the clouds looked ominous. There was promise of rain."

The people on the lifeboat, uncertain when or if they would be rescued, groped through the craft's compartments, searching for food, water and safety gear. They found a lamp, one container of oil, a single can of flares, matches and a lonely tin of biscuits to be divided among the 23 frightened, hungry people adrift on a dark and cold sea.

CHAPTER 1
At Gonzaga

The Jesuit priests at Gonzaga College in Washington, D.C., saw something in Raphael Floyd Gibbons that made them want to educate the boy without charge. He had won no academic scholarship, yet perhaps verve, some spark, a dash of charm or wit shone through—even at age 11.

School records show that the boy's mother, Emma, registered him one day in 1898. Beside his name was the notation that he was the recipient of the Mrs. John Tynan scholarship, an unannounced and otherwise unlisted endowment for just such a young man.

Gibbons' upwardly mobile parents wanted the best for their eldest child, but neither Emma and Edward Gibbons nor young Gibbons could have imagined the rigors of his first year at Gonzaga College, later Gonzaga College High School, by then situated for nearly 30 years in a warren of buildings at 19 Eye Street, NW.

As a matriculating student in what the Jesuits then called the 3rd Academic (completion of three academics meant entrance to the College level), young Gibbons came under the Jesuit *Ratio Studiorum*, or principles of study. As the school catalog of the day stated with accuracy and a degree of arrogance: "It is no mere educational experiment like most of the modern systems. For over one hundred years, it was the only system of Christian education in Europe and most of the great thinkers and writers were brought up under its influence."

His parents, who likely had sent their son previously to public school, were not alone in wishing the best education for him. Irish, German and Italian middle and working class parents made great sacrifices to cover the yearly $40 tuition at Gonzaga so their boys could join the school's alumni, who were the Capital city's businessmen, government clerks, doctors, lawyers and priests. Gibbons' own class at

Floyd Gibbons, age 20, grew up on 14th St NW, Washington, D.C., attended Gonzaga College, moved west and later attended Georgetown College. His father was a restless egg and butter salesman with an entrepreneurial streak. His mother was a milliner. Floyd was the oldest of five.

Gonzaga[1] would produce at least one cleric, the Rev. Arthur O'Leary, S.J., who became president of Georgetown College, while an older schoolmate, the Rev. William C. Repetti, became Georgetown's archivist and keeper of alumni records. Wrote Repetti on Gibbons' alumni card: "Attended Gonzaga before coming to Georgetown. He was always a cocky little fellow."

The Gonzaga Gibbons entered displayed its own brand of underdog cockiness. A move from its central location at 10th and F Streets NW in 1871 left the school far fewer students in what was still largely an undeveloped area of North Capitol and Eye streets, known as Swampoodle, where cows grazed in the Capitol's shadow. The Jesuits had moved the school next door to the Society's 12-year-old Church of St. Aloysius, but had not been able to persuade much of the student body to come along. Enrollment went from an average in recent years of 150 to 70. A severe recession, the loss of all Jesuit scholastics to a new centralized seminary, plus the chaos and mud of Washington's first large scale street and sewer construction didn't help matters either. Even so, the Jesuits pressed on. Losing money—never a favorite practice of the Society of Jesus—and with colleagues at rival Georgetown College, located across town in the old colonial port, pushing to close Gonzaga, the school on Eye Street opted to add military training to its curriculum. This reflected a larger trend in American secondary education as well as being one of several moves to grow enrollment, including offering training for the federal civil service exam and business courses.

In offering uniforms, sabers and close-order drill, the priests were hoping to enhance the school's image and increase enrollment, but the Order had its own military connections some 350 years old. The Jesuits' very founder, St. Ignatius of Loyola, a Spanish knight, began the Order of the Society of Jesus after a post-battlefield conversion. The Order's founding document invites the allegiance of "whoever desires to serve as a soldier of God." To this day, some call the Jesuits "God's Marines" and St. Ignatius is the Catholic Church's patron saint of soldiers.

As early as the school's inaugural year in 1821, when it was called Washington Catholic Seminary and was located at 917 F Street, NW, students marched in military style formations for parades, including one

Floyd Gibbons at age 2. European and American style through the early 20th century was to clothe boys in dresses early in life.

Father Edward T. Gibbons and mother Emma Theresa Gibbons. Both were children of Irish Catholic immigrants.

welcoming the Marquis of Lafayette, the hero of the Revolution, on his visit to the nation he helped establish.

Another military display march was noted by the July 19, 1850, edition of the *National Intelligencer*, whose reporter watched Gonzaga students march to Carusi's theater for their commencement. "The smaller boys appeared in yellow jackets with standing collars, each set off with two golden stars," the journalist reported. "This uniform struck us as highly becoming the little fellows. The second department appeared in a purple color [perhaps then as now honoring the color of the Italian Gonzaga family]; the third in sky blue; the fourth in green; the fifth in dark blue; the sixth in black; the seventh, the senior class, wore black frock coats; all had white pantaloons and glazed caps....We hear but one opinion, that it was the handsomest affair of the kind ever got up in our city."

Students clearly embraced the pageantry and militarism because they formed the school's first cadet corps in 1853 as an extracurricular club. It didn't last long but clearly the interest was there. The overly-ambitious Guards asked Secretary of War Jefferson Davis for actual arms and ammunition. Reported an amused Jesuit diarist that year: "Their ranks have not been seen marshalling in dread array for some days. A scarcity of powder, balls and guns is the alleged cause of this lack of spirit. The Secretary of War has, it seems, thought proper to refuse any thing in the shape of blunderbusses to beardless heroes. This, as might be expected, has made him unfit for the office he fills, at least in the opinion of these juveniles."

The earliest years of Gonzaga saw the sons of prominent military leaders enrolled at the school. Enrollment records show fathers with titles of Captain or Colonel or Commodore before their names. Gonzaga graduates not infrequently received appointments to the Naval Academy and West Point. One Gonzaga President, the Rev. James Clark, S.J., was a classmate of Robert E. Lee when they graduated from West Point in 1829. In antebellum days, two Lee cousins attended Gonzaga. The Civil War offered a counterpoint of reality for any Gonzaga student or Jesuit caught up in the fantasy of military gamesmanship. As soon as secessionist guns fired on federal Fort Sumter, off Charleston, South Carolina, in 1861,

Gonzaga College Cadet Marching Band members. Gibbons began at Gonzaga, then a military school, in September of 1898, part of the class of 1906. The band would play the stirring marches of Marine Band leader John Philip Sousa, who had taught music to the cadets part time.

parents pulled sons from Gonzaga to get them away from the threat of war. Older students withdrew to follow the flag, usually the Confederacy's stars and bars, and during the war the school's enrollment dwindled from a prewar high of 400 to only about 100.

As the Civil War years receded, Catholic education increasingly embraced the military model, adopted from Europe where noble sons not the oldest or the heir often went into uniform. The term "cadet" is from the French for "younger son." Many an educator, Catholic and otherwise, saw multiple benefits to close-order drill and other aspects of military discipline as a means of bringing around sloppy, surly and unkempt striplings.

However, the Jesuits had other purposes, such as exhibited at New York City's Xavier College, where the order adopted military forms to shake off the suggestion that its faculty and students were anything but red-blooded American males.

"In the United States in the 1870s and 1880s, a militaristic patriotism was in the air," it states in *Xavier: Reflections on 150 Years, 1847-1997.*

> "The nation was on the brink of an age of imperialism, which would be expressed, often militarily, in the Spanish-American War, the acquisition of the Philippines, the domination of the Caribbean, and the building of the Panama Canal. At the same time, ideas of manliness were undergoing a change, especially among the educated. No longer was the refined French gentleman the ideal. Manners, devotion, piety and intellectual commitments were no means devalued, but neither were they celebrated as before. The idea of manliness had in a sense been athleticized. A man demonstrated his manliness in athletics, in the military, in competition, in every kind of activity that involved discipline and conquest. The military drill was the perfect way for the Jesuits to march with the times; to show they were patriotic Americans involving men for the future."

At Gonzaga's Diamond Jubilee celebration in 1896, Richmond Bishop John Keane spoke at length of Gonzaga and its military training.

> "Gonzaga College fully appreciates the debt that it owes to the boys, to this external and worldly side of their life. It not only teaches them how to say their prayers and recite their lessons, but, as we have witnessed today, it teaches them how to hold the musket, how to beat the drums, how to sound the horn, how to march in soldierly array. It does not, indeed, wish that her boys should ever shed the blood of their fellow men. But she does wish that if the need should ever come her boys should stand among the foremost in fighting for country laying down their lives for fatherland."

With young Gibbons looking sharp in his new uniform, the Gibbonses sent their son to the demanding Jesuits in the fall of 1898. His schedule was an intense one, but included breaks. Boys had Thursdays and Sundays off, as well as certain holidays, holy days and eight weeks of summer. On March 17 and June 21, the feasts of Saints Patrick and Aloysius, school closed, reflecting a heavy Hibernian enrollment and the wish to honor the school's namesake.

Otherwise, the school day began with Mass at 8:30 a.m. and included a brief morning recess and a longer lunch break. Dismissal came at 2:30. That 8:30 Mass might have been tough for young Gibbons, whose family lived more than 20 blocks away at 1535 14th Street, NW. His father, to assure his mischievous boy got to school on time, likely chauffeured him as part of his egg and butter delivery route.

Gibbons was in the A section of Third Academic and his book bag must have sagged. The curriculum he encountered was extremely demanding.

His name doesn't appear in the honor rolls that year and it likely presaged the academic ennui he encountered later with the Jesuits at Georgetown College. As his younger brother wrote some years later: "It has always been a wonder to me that Floyd didn't suffer either from fallen arches or mental exhaustion from studying all those subjects...."[2]

However Gibbons may have prospered or suffered academically at Gonzaga, his maiden aunt was more than pleased to see her nephew get a Catholic education, a cause she had been pressing for years. "Have you had a chance to call on... [priests] in reference to Floyd's schooling?" an anxious Anne Phillips wrote her sister Emma in 1893. "Do attend to this matter at once. It is of the greatest importance. He will never amount to anything if you permit him to run the streets all day and school is the place for him. After school hours for Lord's sake keep him indoors, away from bad company. You know he is just at that age when he will learn everything (bad especially) and those boys around are, I think, too old in every way for six-year-old Floyd." Gibbons so loved that letter he had it framed.

Amid such academic demands, young Gibbons must have enjoyed stretching his muscles while marching on the Eye Street parade grounds. Add to that physical stimulus the drums and brass of the Gonzaga military band, once led by U.S. Marine Band Conductor John Phillip Sousa, and playing the soul-stirring marches that made Sousa a household name. The band and cadets marched in the Inaugural Parade of William McKinley in 1897. How could an adolescent like Gibbons not love the military?

While attending Gonzaga, Gibbons landed his first job--an experience that would resonate for the rest of his life and that might also help explain his absence from the school honor rolls. He became a *Washington Post* newsboy and each evening would pick up a stack of early editions to peddle for pennies per copy in the classic newsboy mode. The U.S. had gone to war with Spain and readers were hungry for the latest reports from Cuba and the Philippines. Gibbons delighted in being part of the war excitement and would stay out as late as 2 a.m. to hawk the extra *Post* editions declaring "AMERICAN CITIZENS IN DANGER" or asking "WILL IT BE WAR."

For Gibbons the man, it would always be war.

CHAPTER 2
Young Floyd

Raphael Floyd Phillips Gibbons was born in his parents' bed on July 16, 1887, in Washington, D.C., eldest of the five children of Edward T. and Emma Gibbons. His paternal grandparents, John and Mary Gibbons, had come to the U.S. from Ireland in 1856 and settled in the old port district of Georgetown. The 1880 Census lists John as working at a restaurant and shows Edward, 20, employed as a barkeeper. At some point John Gibbons started a real estate business and "became fairly prosperous," another son wrote.

As soon as Raphael Floyd Gibbons was old enough to stop going by "Raphael," he did. He thought it too effeminate, and its angelic nature may have rubbed him the wrong way. He went instead by his middle name, chosen by his parents to honor a friend. John Floyd Waggaman was a wealthy real estate investor, a man the elder Gibbonses no doubt hoped their son would emulate in the business world.[3] Gibbons' father was a dapper man who meticulously trimmed his red beard. An ever-optimistic chatterbox, Edward Gibbons was a serial entrepreneur—a natural promoter looking to build a better sales mousetrap or to strike oil.

In one of Edward's earliest ventures, he cast himself as a butter and egg man selling his wares at markets and to housewives on his daily route. To convey the appearance of success—a lifelong habit—Edward painted his only wagon one color on one side and another color on the other side. One side read "EDWARD T. GIBBONS BUTTER AND EGG COMPANY, NORTHEAST MARKET WASHINGTON, D.C. WAGON NUMBER 1." The other side read the same but "WAGON NUMBER 2." To increase sales, Edward published a giveaway gossip sheet, handed out to customers. Some copies included lucky numbers, entitling bearers to free eggs or cheese. The arrangement backfired when a thug showed up with all the winning papers and demanded his winnings. Police were called and the miscreant removed.

While Edward peddled dairy goods, Emma handled the children at several apartments on 14th Street, NW, also working as a milliner. She was ambitious enough to see to it that Floyd and daughter Zelda attended a birthday party in suburban Garrett Park, Md., in 1894, as reported in the social notes of the *Evening Star.*

Many years later, Floyd Gibbons could have been writing of his father's restless entrepreneurship when he returned from Europe after a decade and was comparing the ambitious American worker to his more relaxed European cousin. "Everybody thinks that just ahead is a million dollars. Maybe he is wrong. Maybe it isn't there, but he thinks it is, and that makes him a buyer, he makes the bull market."

It was just that tug at the end of the school year in 1899 that made Edward uproot his family and move to Des Moines, Iowa, where he hoped to make his million in trading stamps. He convinced retailers to buy the stamps from him and give them out along with purchases to customers who in turn could use them to get other goods free.

Edward's vivacity was difficult to resist. "With a twinkle in his eye, his red whiskers flared out, and fresh as result of his sixth shirt of the day, no one could ever accuse him of being downhearted. Floyd in later years would develop much the same characteristics," wrote Floyd Gibbons' brother, Edward. [4]

In Des Moines his father encouraged Gibbons to take up public speaking and acting. He built a collapsible platform on which his son could stage Wild West plays and do his impression of Teddy Roosevelt, his hero. Gibbons became an actual hero one day when he saved his brother Edward from drowning in the Des Moines River, a show of fearlessness that would become his hallmark.

The trading stamp business was doing so well for the senior Gibbons that in 1901 he expanded his territory to Minneapolis and moved the family to that city. Feeling flush, he organized the Big Four Oil Company, based in Beaumont, Texas. He sold shares and obtained leases. Ever the optimist, he held a grand party on June 24, 1902, inviting all of

Beaumont to a free stage play. Everyone who came received a free share in his oil company. Beaumont had to like this flamboyant salesman.

The launch was a hit, but not the wells. When oil finally did gush, years later, it came too late for the Gibbons family.

But the trading stamp operation flourished, and when young Gibbons had advanced further in school, his parents sent him back to Washington and the Jesuits, this time to Washington's Georgetown College, where in 1905 Gibbons not only flunked Latin, Greek and English but joined fellow dormitory residents in a sit-down strike against oppressive discipline. The young men tossed porcelain washbasins and pitchers from windows and flooded the dorm's second floor with a fire hose.

His son's hand in the ruckus brought his father a bill for $250, no doubt prompting a meaningful exchange between father and son. Further vexing the Jesuit fathers, Gibbons and a co-conspirator spread flypaper on the floor just inside a dining room. Soon men in cassocks were hopping madly about with papers stuck to their feet. Gibbons' rap sheet came to include running naked in a hazing incident, shooting craps and being at hand when someone set fire to a fence separating the all-male Georgetown College from the all-female Georgetown Visitation school.

Homesickness and Jesuit discipline no doubt contributed to his misbehavior. In February, 1906, Emma Gibbons had visited her boy. Afterward, in a letter to his father, Gibbons noted his mother left at noon that day. "...And after seeing her off I certainly felt as that the light had gone out and things were dark once more for I know I miss her lots because I have had such a fine time while she has been here, being able to get out any time and have been treated to some swell freedom." It's no wonder Gibbons tells his father he is "not feeling well." Academic failure and behavior problems surely were taking their toll. And as seen from an earlier letter, his father is not the one to look for consolation. His father wrote him Nov. 17, and there is an underlying anger throughout.

Dear Floyd: Yours of Nov 9th received. Glad to hear from you but sorry you can not find the opportunity to write us more frequently. I would sincerely suggest, knowing that you do know how interested we are, in your doings, that you buy yourself a large tablet and jag down at stated intervals each day matters that you know it is of interest here and set some proper time each week to finish same and mail to us…I am also sorry to hear that some of your Georgetown College boys have not conducted themselves along the proper lines in some of their visits to the city….

I am going to ask you as of most vital importance outside of yourself from one who has your future interest most at heart, that you cut away from any of the coarse or rude and unrefined associates and try to select as your friends and companions that is an elevation rather than a deteriorate to you…. Also, one other thing I want to emphatically bury in your memory chambers is that if you want to please me and all others that are interested in you, that you make a positive promise in your next letter in answer to this that you will carry out, keep out of all saloons, either as a patronizer, looker on, or a companion of others, as you know there is none of us that places ourselves in the way of temptation but is apt to fall…."

In the letter, his father also expressed anger that the young man had not called on several people his dad had insisted he meet, including Gibbons' uncle John. Edward then told young Gibbons he wanted him to work on the college paper "as it would give us great pleasure to read some of your compositions which we know you have the ability along the original lines in print." He told Gibbons he also wanted him to take up an instrument or singing and "some literary or social society there."

The two college letters portray a parents'-eye view of a rebellious, alienated, non-communicative student, and, as the year went on, Gibbons became depressed. Georgetown gave him the gate and he headed home.

His academic career a disaster--Gibbons said classroom teaching bored him--he returned to Minneapolis. He landed a job in a coal yard in Lucca, North Dakota, shoveling coal and stacking lumber. Nights he got on at a local print shop that published a weekly, his first adult glimpse of serious newspapering. He returned to Minneapolis, where he tried selling electric cars and helped with the trading stamp business until he persuaded his father to let him see if he could pursue a job at the *Minneapolis Daily News* as a reporter, a trade the senior Gibbons greatly feared. "I don't want any son of mine to become a newspaper reporter and grow up to be a drunken bum," his brother quoted his father as saying.

Despite his father's resistance, or because of it, Gibbons contacted the paper, was offered a position, and jumped at the opportunity to make $7 a week learning to report and write routine stories. "One day he would be recording a police-station scene while a little girl was telling of the death of a dog under the wheels of her car; the next he would be reporting how a scrubwoman deposited a thousand dollars as bail for her son, who had robbed a safe," his brother wrote, "The third day it would be a confession from one of a gang of car robbers."

His name debuted above a story he wrote about a Turk applying for American citizenship. The copy desk had given it a thorough going over.

Said Gibbons: "My first thrill was seeing my by-line for the first time in the *Minneapolis Daily News*. I had written a ponderous story, pathos and bathos about a Turk who had applied for American citizenship papers and claimed he could read, but when pressed for proof admitted he could only read the advertisements of Turkish cigarettes. Naturally, when I found the story, it had been boiled down to seven lines, but it still was my by-line and that gave me a tremendous kick."

Gibbons found he was completely in his element. The newsroom's sudden eruptions from placidity into manic energy delighted him. He loved the elation particular to the young journalist who gets to learn something no one else knows and tells it to the world--or at least the greater Minneapolis area. The *News* was a morning paper; its staff worked evenings. At home, Gibbons would talk at length with his mother about the stories he was writing, and they would go over different angles and contexts, chats he said that very much improved his skills.

While his mother was encouraging him, his father wanted him to quit, which he would not do. His father even confronted his son's editor, William Shepherd, and demanded that he be fired. Shepherd refused, stating Gibbons "has a natural nose for news." Even so, before long Shepherd did fire the younger Gibbons over a botched assignment or blown deadline. "You ought to go to Timbuctu and learn how to be a reporter," he told Gibbons before he just as quickly rehired him. Years later, on assignment in Africa and arriving at Timbuctu, Gibbons made a joyful point of sending a telegram to his ex-boss saying he had arrived—as instructed.

While at the *Daily News* from 1907 to 1909, he took a side job as press agent for the Dewey Theater, a vaudeville venue—a firing offense today, but business as usual then. The Dewey paid him with two passes per week, in addition to the shows he would write about. He used the byline "Kate Dean" for his show coverage in the *Daily News*, perhaps thinking a female name would lend credibility to the theater writings. Serving two masters, he polished his prose and became savvier about show business and audiences—lessons he would use throughout his career.

In time, the *Minneapolis Tribune*, which paid better, hired Gibbons from the *News*. His star rose quickly there, garnering him entrée to a major story that made his early career—and landed him behind bars.

CHAPTER 3
The Battle of Cameron Dam

In Wisconsin, Winter was not only a long, hard season but the name of a remote town of fewer than 100 souls. One-hundred-and-fifty miles northeast of Minneapolis, Winter got its name from an Omaha Railroad official who helped start the village by bringing his company's single track rail line there to ship out the old growth white pine. The Iroquois called it the Tree of Peace and prized it as sacred; white men paid dearly for its clear, strong wood.

Lumberjacks had been felling trees near Winter for 75 years. The Wisconsin pinery was nearly logged out and everybody was trying to wring every dime possible from the vanishing forest. Others, like reporter Floyd Gibbons, would find their careers boosted in the final days of the old growth pine.

The woods in northern Wisconsin had succeeded the Northeast as lumberyard for the frontier in the 1840s as settlers moved to the Midwestern prairies. Trees grew to a height of 150 feet in the North Country and weatherproof and straight-grained white pine was converted to joists, beams, flooring and laths, furniture, implements and the wagons that made for the settlement of the Midwest up to the Rockies. One tree could yield 5,000 board feet of lumber, and the Wisconsin pinery between 1875 and 1900 yielded 52 billion board feet. Lumbermen saw it as limitless. As Frederick Weyerhaeuser, who founded the monolithic eponymous lumber concern, liked to say: "You have to have a crib for every baby that is born and a box when you carry him out."

After the Civil War, big business and veterans flocked to the woods to make their fortune. In the ensuing years, the state case law and legislation of damming rights, rights of way and timber and river rights were hammered out, and as Weyerhaeuser and its subsidiaries expanded, Frederick Weyerhaeuser and his lawyers typically kept a possessive eye on the region's rivers and timber roads. But these rights were not always as settled as they appeared, as *Tribune* reporter Gibbons would learn.

From Winter, lumbermen could ship logs by rail to a mill 63 miles away in Chippewa Falls, but the cheaper means was to float them down the Brunet or Thornapple rivers that flowed into the larger Chippewa River that ran past the mill. The Thornapple River route, some 40 miles as the crow flies, was simple enough. Along the Thornapple, the Chippewa Lumber and Boom Company, an arm of the Weyerhaeuser conglomerate, built a series of small earthen dams, like one at Cameron 25 feet across and 15 feet high, behind which water and logs collected. Woodsmen would fell and limb trees, leverage them onto horse-drawn sleds or wagons and drop them by the nearest dam. When the harvest had reached critical mass and was ready to sluice to the mill, workers along the chain of dams opened the flood gates. Torrents of water lifted and propelled the wood, urged along by men with picks and peaveys.

The process was interrupted in 1904 when the Dietz clan moved to their 160 acres along the Thornapple--a stretch that, except during the spring flood, was more creek than river.

The family, headed by John Dietz, a stubborn, cantankerous man of German descent, considered anyone setting foot on their land to be trespassing. The same held for using "their" piece of the river. When Dietz bought the land, its deed had been mistakenly filed without all the longstanding right-of-way, flow-through and damming rights. As John Dietz saw it, if the Chippewa Lumber and Boom Company, which had once employed him as a dam watchman, wanted to float logs down his stretch of the Thornapple, the company would have to do two things: Compensate him the $1,700 he claimed the company owed him in back pay for 854 days of work, and pay him 10 cents per thousand board feet for timber that passed his property.

The lumber company might have first sensed something was amiss several weeks earlier when they sent a letter to Dietz telling him to discuss the matter of his wages with John Mulligan, foreman of the Chippewa Lumber Company, at the Cameron Dam site. Even after Dietz showed him the letter, Mulligan flatly refused to even discuss the back pay issue.

An enraged Dietz thrashed the lumberman who filed an assault and battery complaint.

But the lumber company first heard of Dietz's complete demands in April 1904 when crews came to open Cameron Dam to send a load of logs downstream. The men found a hand scrawled sign:

NO TRESPASS

All persons are strictly forbidden trespassing on the N ½ of SW ¼ and S ½ of NW ¼ Sec. 20-38-4W, at their peril

John Dietz

Standing beside the placard was its author pointing a .30-30 Winchester. The lumberjacks were dumbstruck: the dam had been in use since the state legislature authorized its construction in 1874. Tying up Cameron Dam could curtail or hinder logging the full length of the Thornapple. Dietz explained his terms and declared that unless the company met them, no logs would be floating from the dam, which he said lay partly on his property.

Seeing Dietz's violent resolve, the lumber company got his agreement to survey the property, presuming it would prove it owned the dam. Company surveyor Thomas Sargent discovered part of the dam was indeed on the Dietz land and each side agreed to leave the logs and water above the dam until the company could respond to the situation. A week later, Sargent returned and offered Dietz $500 to resolve the matter. An insulted Dietz emphatically told Sargent that this was inadequate. Chippewa Lumber and Boom Company went to Judge John K. Parish, of the state 15th judicial circuit, to plead its case. The judge ordered Dietz to appear and show why he should not be enjoined from holding up the Thornapple logging. On April 27, Sheriff Charles Person served the notice. Dietz ignored it and would claim ever after that Person had not served notice properly.

Obstinate and belligerent as he was, Dietz was no fool. He appeared to have a case, however shaky. And he had been reading the

John Dietz and family, of Cameron Dam, Wis. The combative Dietz and his family resisted authorities for years over property and logging rights in the pine woods of Wisconsin. Gibbons in 1910 was the only reporter at the Dietz homestead when all hell broke loose, once again getting an exclusive story for the Minneapolis Tribune. *His aggressive reporting tactics, however, left him briefly in jail, but they won him the admiration of fellow newsmen.*

writings of Eugene Debs and fellow radicals of the day, as well as the works of progressives like Wisconsin Governor Robert "Fighting Bob" La Follette. Inspired by their rhetoric and by the profit motive, Dietz stood firm. In such episodes no one lost points for stubbornness.

Within days of their father's receipt of the judge's order, Dietz's sons Clarence and Leslie partially raised the dam's gates. That drained the accumulated water but stranded some five million board feet of lumber in the form of 5,000 logs now grounded in a marsh upstream of Cameron Dam. On May 3, Deputy Sheriff Fred Clark called on Dietz to serve papers requiring he come to court. Clark warned Dietz big trouble was coming soon if he didn't. Five days later a wagon carrying Deputy Sheriffs William Giblin and William Elliot, farmhand Erwin Giauque and Chippewa Lumber and Boom representatives John Mulligan and Pat Magin headed towards Dietz's place. The lawmen planned to arrest him. As they neared Dietz's property Dietz and neighbor Valentine Weisenbach jumped from the woods. "Hands up, you sons of bitches!" Dietz yelled. He and Weisenbach opened fire. Four bullets hit the wagon and occupants, one breaking Magin's forearm, another perforating another man's hat. The posse escaped when their wagon's horse team spooked and ran pell mell down the road. Tempting fate the very next day, Deputy Giblin sat at lunch with loggers in a lumber company shanty near the dam well within Dietz rifle range. Someone opened fire, breaking the arm of one logger and grazing another. The lumber company recalled all loggers from the site and marched to see Judge Parish again. Parish declared the lumber company had as much right to "operate the dam and control it, as a man has the right to use his own horse or cow....The defendant has no defense as far as this court is concerned...he has absolutely refused to appear in court for any relief under any pretended claim...."

Parish then perpetually enjoined Dietz from "in any manner interfering with the plaintiffs or their assigns in operating the dam...." Even as the judge was moving against Dietz civilly, the Sawyer County District Attorney's Office was preparing criminal warrants charging Dietz and Weisenbach with intent to murder. Attempts to serve them bore no fruit. By July the manager of Chippewa Lumber, William Irvine, had succeeded in getting a meeting with Dietz. Irvine approached Dietz as

Freemason to Freemason, proposing to turn the matter over to the Grand Mason of Wisconsin, who would appoint several past grand masters to make a binding ruling. The company promised to abide by the Masonic decision and pay Dietz's expenses. Dietz said no. By 1905, state officials and legislators were talking about sending in militia and writing new laws to deal with Dietz, but Dietz and his kidnapped logs, now losing their bark, remained in place.

Backwoods Wisconsin handled legal matters Wild West style. To enforce civil or criminal actions such as these against Dietz, Sheriff James Gylland had to enlist a posse. However, no one in or around Winter wanted to go toe-to-toe with John Dietz, particularly on behalf of Weyerhaeuser.

On April 13, 1906, a brave federal marshal attempted to serve Dietz, but was allowed to come only up to a pile of lumber. He put the oilcloth-wrapped stack of criminal and civil warrants on the wood. Dietz feared the package might be a bomb. "I thought it might possibly be an infernal machine," he said, "so I took a pitchfork and threw it into the river." A week later someone surreptitiously closed the Cameron Dam gates while someone upriver opened the gates of another dam. The surge overflowed the Cameron Dam, weakening it considerably. Its west side collapsed, allowing the river to carry two and a half million board feet of logs towards Chippewa Falls, leaving the other half of the logs stranded in the forest and marsh adjacent to the dam. The two sides blamed each other and the logjam continued.

Dietz's neighbor Weisenbach meanwhile gave himself up. On May 9, 1906 jurors convicted him of attempted murder; a judge sentenced him to 12 years in prison. Six weeks later Sheriff Gylland, unable to gather his posse, hired Milwaukee toughs he dressed in borrowed state militia uniforms. They crept up on the Dietz camp and fired. Clarence was shot, a bullet creasing his scalp. Dietz returned fire, wounding his son's assailant, John Rogisch, in the ankle, buttock and neck. Rogisch and the posse retreated, and once again, the Sheriff, the Judge, and the District Attorney stewed over what to do with John Dietz. The Sawyer County Board, feeling impotent about arresting Dietz, authorized a $500 bounty to bring him in. Someone, anyone, they seemed to be saying, please do something. Nothing was done, until some four years later.

The Minneapolis and Milwaukee papers, including the *Tribune*, Gibbons' employer, gave the violent confrontations considerable attention, and on Aug. 6 the *Milwaukee Journal* asked readers their opinion on "What should be done with John Dietz?" The letters overwhelmingly supported the aggrieved landowner, common remarks being "leave him alone" and "pay him all they owe him." One writer compared upstate law enforcement to a "band of Cossacks." Another wrote: "You have hung one John Brown, don't hang another."

Dietz delighted in the attention. He stoked the fires by writing to the local newspapers. "… [M]yself and family have been the targets for conspiracy, blackmailing and bullets of the land pirates and timber wolves," he wrote in a communiqué published by the *Osceola Sun* in 1907. "Now, dear reader, isn't this a great condition to rear a family of children under in a land of liberty? If such a state of affairs is allowed to continue, the stars and stripes should be hung at half mast to mourn the death of our nation, for the grasping tentacles of the corporation has liberty by the throat." Dietz, who considered himself a poet, sent newspapers his doggerel mocking lumber interests and law enforcement. He held himself up as a socialist and revolutionary, no less significant than three union leaders charged with murdering an ex-governor of Idaho.

> *Men whose honor is above the glitter of*
> *Gold —*
> *Men marked for slaughter who cannot be bought and sold —*
> *Such men are Haywood, Pettibone, Moyer and Dietz*
> *It is high time, my American brother, to sever the chains of*
> *bondage from one to another,*
> *And turn the guiltless out of prison —*
> *Such is the message of Socialism.*

By the fall of 1907, the captive logs were almost completely debarked. It would not be long before insects rendered them useless.

Facing that calamity, Chippewa Lumber and John Dietz each put principles aside. Dietz was offered and accepted his $1,717 in back pay plus any logs left on his property. In exchange, the lumber company could now have access to its logs. With the dam ruined, the Chippewa Lumber workers began the labor-intensive tasks of transporting the lumber left on its property overland to the Flambeau River. Dietz in 1909 contracted to have a portable mill saw his logs.

After resolving the fate of the stranded logs, the lumber company offered to purchase Dietz's farm for $10,000 to $15,000. Few were talking about rebuilding the dam because the pinery was all but gone and roads now crisscrossed the area for whatever gleaning that could be done. Perhaps the lumber concern simply wanted to help remove a nuisance they helped create. Dietz wanted $25,000 and the negotiations stopped.

Dietz had so cowed the authorities that from 1907 to 1910 he and his relations routinely went into Winter to buy supplies and visit neighbors as if Dietz had no warrants for his arrest. The family rarely went unarmed; Dietz wore a Luger on his belt. Daughter Myra must have enjoyed the easing of tensions because she began a column for the *Sawyer County Gazette* covering social news, including the "Sundaying" of the Dietz clan with neighbors. Dietz himself stopped writing to the papers.

With something like peace along the Thornapple, the Winter School Board, at John Dietz's urging, supplied a teacher to live with the Dietz clan to teach the youngest children.

That arrangement led to bloodshed. On Sept. 6, 1910, Dietz and his adult sons Clarence and Leslie came to town to vote in a primary election. In town Clarence saw school board member Charles O'Hare and told him he had heard rumors the board planned to pull its teacher. O'Hare bristled and asked Clarence why it was his business. Clarence was vexed in return and John Dietz jumped into the verbal fray, which quickly became physical. A big logger named Bert Horel threw in on the side of the educator. Pulling his pistol, John Dietz shot Horel in the neck, seriously wounding him. The Dietzes jumped into their wagon and whipped their horses home while rattled authorities once again pondered what to do with the clan.

After simmering for six years, the situation in Winter had reached a peak of tension and violence.

When Dietz fired his pistol that day, Gibbons was enjoying his work as a police beat reporter for the *Minneapolis Tribune*, probing the seamy side of the Twin Cities life and getting notice for his off-beat stories and unusual assignments. At 23, he was out-running, out-reporting, and out-scooping newshawks much his senior. It was no surprise to him or his colleagues that the he got the call to get up to Winter and report on the latest Dietz eruption.

Gibbons reached Winter the weekend of Oct. 1, 1910, after traveling the bumpy timber trails and a rough rail line that made Winter accessible. The Indian summer weekend was sunny and warm, but snow was not far off. Winter was "a primitive north woods logging village of about 80 people on the branch line of a single-track logging railroad," Gibbons wrote. The streets were mud; walking along them meant threading a course between the rear ends of hobbled horses and mules. Gibbons rented a room at the crude Hotel Winter, whitewashed and built hard by an alley. He arranged for a horse to get to the Dietz enclave. As a newsman he would have checked in with the telegraph operator and located Winter's only telephone at the grocery store—for without these tools he couldn't file a scoop. He mounted his rented horse, looking every bit the city slicker in his dark suit and fedora. In town, new acquaintances had warned him not to be cavalier about the Dietzes, and as he counted off the 10 miles of the trek east to the Dietz farm, he must have called out now and then to avoid startling anyone with an itchy trigger finger. When he arrived on site, John Dietz himself came out, whereupon Gibbons laid on the snake oil that is the reporter's mainstay. He made sure that Dietz knew his name and which paper he worked for, explaining that he wanted the good people of Minneapolis to hear John's story as only he could tell it. The son of a business drummer, Gibbons had long since mastered the art of persuasion, and the Dietzes made him welcome.

Inside Dietz's cabin, Gibbons saw a well-used typewriter, a Victrola, an organ, and bookshelves lined with works by muckraking reporters and radicals like Eugene Debs. As the newsman was sowing the seeds of commonality with his subject, however, trouble was accumulating.

Dietz had been planning to go into town for supplies with his oldest sons. The trip was delayed when Gibbons showed up, and Dietz told Clarence, 23, and Leslie, 20, to head out. Myra, 21, asked if she could now take her father's seat and climbed aboard. Clarence drove the two colts that pulled the springed wagon, and as they headed into Winter the men checked that their guns were loaded.

In Winter, new Sheriff Mike Madden had deputized a tough storekeeper and another man known as a marksman. Both likely were more interested in the bounty on Dietz, now up to $1,000, than upholding the law. Madden had hoped to deputize more men, but nobody else wanted any part of his enterprise.

Madden and his deputies hid behind windfalls and brush some four miles from where Gibbons and Dietz were chatting on the Dietz farm. When the Dietz wagon appeared, the sheriff and his men opened fire, wounding Clarence and Myra. With bullets whipping past, Leslie escaped and made for home. Out of breath after his sprint, Leslie yelled to his father and an astonished Gibbons that he did not know what had become of his brother and sister. "They got us," he cried hysterically. "They just opened fire!"

Reporters like Gibbons live for moments like these. Gibbons was about to hightail it to the telegraph office to file when an enraged John Dietz stopped him. He had a message for Sheriff Madden: "Tell him I'm coming in to get my boy and girl if I have to shoot my way."

Ecstatic at being in the middle of a huge breaking story, Gibbons lashed his horse like the rental it was. When he reached Winter, he quickly dictated a story filled with exclusive quotes from the Dietzes and details no other reporter had. As he filed, the town was in tumult. Sheriff Madden declared martial law, closed the saloons and deputized scores of men to patrol the town and keep a lookout for Dietz. The shooting of an unarmed woman provoked outrage across the Midwest. A flurry of editorials condemned the actions, including one by *the St. Paul Dispatch*

Gibbons in the woods near Cameron Dam.

mockingly suggesting Sheriff Madden employ a mortar to level the Dietz cabin. A torrent of letters enveloped Wisconsin officialdom. Governor James Davidson dispatched Attorney General Frank Gilbert to see if he could settle the matter. By now, Sheriff Madden had deputized 100 men, including many locals concerned for their own safety. Madden had confined Clarence Dietz in the town hall, and made sure the doctor stowed sister Myra at Hotel Winter--in a room next to the one Gibbons was renting.

Once the *Tribune* ran Gibbons' scoop and other papers around the country picked the story up, Winter was awash in newsmen smelling blood and printer's ink. One of these was the enterprising Jack "Red" Schwartz of the *Minneapolis Journal*, Gibbons' main competitor from the Twin Cities. The hundred deputies had on their heels a pack of at least 25 reporters as they prepared to take the war to Dietz before he could bring it to town. Hotel Winter, booked to capacity, now had only its wood floors to rent, and men slept shoulder to shoulder nightly at a buck and a half each. Throughout Oct. 6, 7 and 8, deputies, reporters and gapers rode horses, wagons and buckboards out to the edges of the Dietz place. Both sides kept binoculars and wary eyes on each other.

In his reporting for the *Tribune*, Gibbons painted a sharp contrast between lawmen on alert and the Dietz cabin, from which he could hear sacred music.

"Grim deputies, wrapped in their peajackets, some on blankets, rest on their guns," wrote Gibbons. "Across the scene of the days' expected conflict floated the strains of an organ and voices chanting 'Jesus, Lover of My Soul.' It was the morning prayer. Many of the deputies bared their heads...."

Hiding among the hardwoods and brush, and boxing the farm in on all sides but the south, the deputies called for Dietz, wife Hattie, son Leslie and the youngest kids, Helen and Johnny, to come out. Dietz refused. The posse emptied rifles into the Dietz cabin. Defenders huddled out of range in a cellar dug for this purpose.

As the lawmen and the Dietz clan hunkered down in the standoff, Gibbons and his rival Red Schwartz raced from the site at deadline to beat each other.

On the day after his earlier scoop, Gibbons lost to the speedier Schwartz and Gibbons was bawled out by his what-have-you-done-for-me-lately editor. Gibbons wasn't going to let that happen again. But Red Schwartz intended to see that it did via a devious plan that luckily Gibbons had figured out.

To foil his competitor, Gibbons hired the only car in town, an open-air Rambler, and paid a man to drive it. He offered Schwartz a lift to town where Schwartz quietly had paid a big lumberjack to keep everyone away from Winter's only phone. Schwartz yelled to the big lumberman to connect him with his paper pronto. With that, Gibbons unearthed his surprise –a hidden ax, which he used to cut the phone line, severing the town's sole power line in the process. He had his man run him to the telegraph office, leaving Red Schwartz to get even redder.

That scoop landed Gibbons behind bars. A constable took him before Justice of the Peace W. H. Noyes, who saw to it that the troublemaker was held overnight. "Although Gibbons was now in difficulty in Winter, Wisconsin, he was a hero in Minneapolis," a later account in the *Chicago Tribune* said, "And his editor wired his congratulations on his great scoop. In a few days he was out of jail and able to cover the climax of the siege, John Dietz's surrender to authorities." The *Minneapolis Tribune* paid his fine and gave him a bonus.

Dietz had surrendered after a deputy had been killed. He stood trial for murder and was sentenced to life. After ten years, he was pardoned under public pressure and died in 1924.

Cameron Dam made Gibbons a local star, the *Chicago Tribune* wrote in 1940. "Here was a man who met life with dash and drama and also could never bother with what seemed to him like unimportant details." But to remain a star in what nonetheless was the backwater firmament of Minneapolis, he had to keep delivering scoops.

CHAPTER 4
'The Feeling of Fear'

After Cameron Dam, Gibbons seemed even more determined to get that story—whatever that story was.

Two weeks before Christmas 1910, Gibbons was in the newsroom offices just after midnight when word came of fire at the Hotel Brunswick, a few blocks away at Fourth Street and Hennepin Avenue. The 1872 gabled building was brick, but its interior contained a forest's worth of wood, and flames sent guests and employees scrambling into the night. The five-story hotel, the town's oldest, had a varied reputation, but it was often known as a trysting place for prominent Twin Cities types. As 150 terrified guests darted down the fire escapes or rode out on firefighters' shoulders, Gibbons, who had sprinted from the *Tribune* office, ran into the lobby. Braving embers and ash and firemen's curses, he went to the main desk, looking for reportorial gold—the guest registry. He grabbed the book and, before the Brunswick could burn like a piece of fireplace fatwood, scampered to his perch in the newsroom to identify those the fire displaced and allow Minneapolis readers the delight in speculating why they had not been in their own beds.

For the same reason he ran to fires, Gibbons loved automobiles, in particular racing cars; they seemed a perfect delivery mechanism for the exhilaration Gibbons craved. In the early 1900s, the internal combustion engine could propel humans at speeds unimaginable only a few years before. Auto racing galvanized the American public. Daredevil speed merchants crisscrossed the country setting and then trying to break speed records without breaking their necks. Since the day the first foot pressed the first pedal to the floorboards, cars made drivers want to see how fast they could go. Previously, the gold standard was the quarter horse, a western breed able to reach 50 miles per hour. In 1898, Count Gaston De Chasselloup-Laubet pushed his chain-driven electrically powered Jeantaud to an unheard of 39 mph along a kilometer stretch of straight, smooth

Gibbons showed his trademark fearlessness and resolve to get the story when he ran into the burning Brunswick Hotel in December 1910 to grab the guest registration book as part of the Minneapolis Tribune's *coverage.*

paved road. Other Europeans in electric vehicles gradually raised the bar several miles an hour yearly until Jan., 12, 1904, when, on behalf of the United States, Henry Ford himself entered the competition at the wheel of his company-built stripped-down wooden-framed, single seat Arrow. Ford broke the record by reaching 91 mph, clocked by the American Automobile Association on a cinder-coated stretch of frozen Lake St. Clair, Mich. Racers like Fred Marriott in his Stanley Rocket and Barney Oldfield and "Wild Bob" Burman in their Blitzen Benzes were as famous as baseball pros after each set a world record on the flat and expansive sands of Daytona Beach, Fla. Burman and his 200 horsepower Benz set a record of 141 mph on April 13, 1910.

Cars were still somewhat of an expensive novelty and the thrill of running one full out was available only to professional drivers and car magnates with no one to answer to but their next of kin. Gibbons yearned to join the elect—and to do so in the company of the man who had traveled faster than any human. On Sept. 9, 1911, the glib newshawk unabashedly courted Burman, in town to race his Blitzen Benz on the oval one-mile dirt Hamline track on the State Fair Grounds in St. Paul.

Burman was favored in the race, so he and Gibbons were forced to watch as the six other racers were given a head start down a track heavy on the sides with ridged mud and surrounded by a white fence. The two adjusted their goggles, tried to breathe through the exhaust and waited fifty seconds before they got the flag.

If anything could be described as the element for which Floyd Gibbons was born, the auto race track was it, and as he would do later in even far more dangerous circumstances, he made sure to note every frightening fact and thought for his readers: "It was just as Bob roared into the quarter. The track was full of ridges and ruts and at every slightest bump the Benz bounded up and at 'em....Hunks of [mud] flew from the [car ahead] and our faces ploughed through the mud-air mixture at the rate of 60 miles-per hour. I stood the pelting as long as I could and then ducked my head, but Wild Bob kept his chin in the flying clods and just let 'er rip."

Burman won the race and Gibbons' prize was the experience and the right to analyze it. "At a velocity greater than a mile a minute, sensations are obviously flitting. So is everything else. It is only on the curves that the nerves and mind concentrate for any period upon one thing. The best way I can express it is 'fighting the outer fence.' That ridge of white wood seems to hold magnetic attraction for every bolt and fiber of the racing machine. The occupants feel the 'pull' the fence exerts.... It is peculiar, but the feeling of fear does not enter, even when the rear wheels begin to creep sideways. Somehow or other it struck me at the time that there would be an awful killing if the fence succeeded in drawing us out onto it.

"On the straightaway the speed sensation is one of glorious exultation. It puts the spirit into a man to stick his chin up and feel the air split on his Adams apple. It is almost conductive to hilarity. There is inclination to throw back the head and laugh, absolutely laugh, while the ground unwinds dizzily beneath the flying wheels and the exhaust pipes spit fire and rattle like the inferno. That is the way it felt to me even if it does sound maniacal. Sitting beside a wild man is not without its influence."

The "pull of the fence" did indeed prove too much for Burman. In a 1916 Corona, Cal. race, his Peugeot rolled, killing him and three spectators.

When Gibbons was not chasing thrills and stories, he worked at improving his skills as a reporter and stylist. His roommate, Jack Jensen, about 25-years Gibbons' senior, was an old-school newsman for the *Tribune*. Gibbons continually pumped Jensen for insights into the trade while Jensen emptied his daily intake of two bottles of liquor. Jensen refused to share. "You're Irish, and you can't drink. I'm a Swede and I can," he told Gibbons.

Gibbons was never fond of literature, but Jensen showed him the English classics and how they could help his writing. Gibbons then saw a practical value and later said he learned to "write by reading."

Where others found terror, Gibbons often found joy. Riding with world auto speed champion Bob Burman in his Blitzen Benz, Gibbons became positively giddy in September 1911 while in a race at the Twin Cities' Hamlin track. Gibbons described "glorious exhilaration" in his report for the Minneapolis Tribune *and recalled the race "conducive of hilarity." As a passenger, Gibbons was in the most dangerous seat in the car because there was nothing to hold onto. Burman died in a race crash in 1916, killing three spectators.*

Jensen did not share Gibbons' journalistic ambition—he preferred the day-to-day *Tribune* reporter's lot of routine police, government and business stories, repeatedly refusing offers to work at bigger papers for bigger salaries. He would not even consider a Minneapolis editorship.

Gibbons was forever chagrined when Jensen died in 1936 and an obituary read: "His claim to fame was that he once roomed with Floyd Gibbons."

Gibbons was far more willing than Jensen to move about, going to the *Milwaukee Free Press*. While there, he scored a scoop by interviewing Bull Moose Presidential candidate Theodore Roosevelt after the former president was wounded in an assassination attempt. His Milwaukee stint was a matter of months, however, because he missed his family in Minneapolis and he got his job back at the *Tribune* cop shop. Gibbons never made much money there and what money he had he quickly spent. Colleagues, competitors, sources and the city's police and firemen remembered Gibbons as a constant cadger of nickels and dimes—always repaid. He was also an easy touch. "Money never gave him serious thought," the *Chicago Tribune* wrote.

His star was on the rise in the small constellation that was Minnesota journalism but one night in 1912 his career there came to an abrupt end. He was on duty but asleep in the City Hall press room when the fire bell began to clang. The noise kept up for 10 straight minutes as every available piece of fire apparatus sped to the downtown blaze. But Gibbons remained out like a light. The next day the *Daily News* had full details, but not the *Tribune*, and his boss sacked him.

It was simply fatigue that kept him in his slumber, the *Chicago Tribune* wrote in 1940, and Gibbons wrote in the '30s of being fired for sleeping too much. "There are plenty of times we get fired for real shortcomings. For instance, I like to sleep late myself—and have—to disastrous results."

But was he only sleeping? Fires are catnip for reporters; a whiff of smoke and a siren are usually enough to send them screaming out of the blocks, bent on getting a scoop in what may be a life-or-death situation.

Gibbons never said so, but to have missed a fire story, he had to have been drunk. In an article for *Cosmopolitan Magazine* about 20 years later, Gibbons, mindful that more than 20 percent of workers were idle recalled what it was like getting fired. "It is about the most vacant feeling a man ever had," he said. "Seems to me the worst thing about being fired is that a person is plunged into complete idleness and uselessness." He admitted the *Minneapolis Tribune* had pinkslipped him, diverting him into "shoveling wheat and coal, loading flower and...selling bank safes." He left for Chicago that winter and wound up sleeping on benches in the Windy City's parks. He recovered his equilibrium enough to get on as a reporter with the *Chicago World*, a socialist paper that stayed in print while striking pressmen, stereotypers, deliverymen and mail-drivers shut down the city's other papers in May of 1912. The paper drew a motley assortment of journalists, including one named Carl Sandburg, who went on to win a Pulitzer in poetry. Sandburg years later renewed his friendship with Gibbons in a note by recalling their catnaps in the police headquarters.

When the union strikes ended in November, so too did the *World*, and Gibbons applied to the *Chicago Tribune*. At the interview, he looked more alley-dweller than news-gatherer to reporter Burton Rascoe, who recalled that "...a hulking young fellow come in the office one day...His name was Gibbons, Floyd Gibbons, and he had been working on a socialist paper which had suddenly folded up.... This Gibbons had been on his uppers for some time. He hadn't shaved for a day or two and he looked like a bum. His clothes were a fright--unpressed and greasy as anything. His old boss on the Socialist paper was head of the copy desk at the *Tribune* then and he got Gibbons a job. Gibbons asked for a salary advance—which wasn't much—and went out to get himself cleaned up and to buy himself a suit.... He went to a barber and to a Turkish bath.... Gibbons emerged from this ordeal with the gosh-awfulest suit I ever saw on a human being outside of a burlesque house."

Gibbons had the fellow *Tribune* reporters smirking at his appearance, but his reporting quickly squared things away. Competing papers liked his work, and Hearst's *Examiner* stole him with a good raise. Stung at losing a comer, *Tribune* editor Walter Howe got him back after only two weeks with an even larger salary.

Gibbons was assigned to a *Tribune* muckraking effort at exposing medical quackery. An unemployed man reported going to a drugstore to buy exercise equipment only to be snookered by a hustler behind the counter. The con man convinced the fellow he could be at death's door and needed a checkup. The grifter "examined" the mark and hustled him out the door with a bottle of pills and $12 less than he had had when he came in. A buddy steered the sucker to the *Tribune*, which put Gibbons on the case. Posing as a rube, Gibbons went to the same store saying he was after gym gear. He got the same runaround, including the incisive medical question: "Do you feel sleepy when you wake up?" Oh yes, said Gibbons, whereupon his interviewer told him to thank his lucky stars for coming into the store. Same exam, same sugar pills, same $12 invoice. However, Gibbons filed a complaint with the police and swore out a warrant for the man's arrest, then buttonholed the organizer of the three-store scam and asked for his medical credentials. "Don't you think we are doing a lot for the service of humanity?" the con artist asked.

"Doc, I think you are the darnedest bunch of crooks unhung in this country," Gibbons replied.

Gibbons also filed a complaint about the organizer. Early the next morning, he traveled to the Chicago slammer to interview the store clerk, who had just awakened. "Tell me, did you feel sleepy when you woke up this morning?" Gibbons asked.

By now, Gibbons was getting used to being an ace reporter. But he wanted his pay to reflect it and demanded more. Howe balked and either Gibbons quit or was fired after not getting a bump.

If unemployment weren't enough, Gibbons impetuously on Feb. 5th, 1914, married Isabela C. Pehrman, a tall 22-year-old former stenographer and bookkeeper at Minneapolis' Abbott Hospital, a match he came to regret.

Newly married and utterly broke, Gibbons' prospects and timing seemed questionable as he and his bride moved into an apartment at 4239 Kenmore Ave., Chicago. A lawyer friend offered Gibbons work in public relations and fund-raising for Carl Person, a Machinists Union editor accused of murdering Tony Musser, an ex-sheriff in downstate Illinois. Musser on Dec. 30, 1913, jumped the much-smaller Person as part of a campaign to force an end to a two-year-old Illinois Central railroad strike. Person shot and killed Musser and was jailed. The resulting murder case became a cause célèbre among leftists and organized labor supporters. Gibbons tried his hand at propaganda, writing up the case for the *International Socialist Review*, publisher of Jack London, Upton Sinclair and Eugene Debs. Gibbons cast Person against the Illinois Central Railroad Goliath. "It makes the red blood leap and bound to watch the struggle," he wrote. "It makes the heart choke and stop at the thought of the consequences, should the Giant land one of his mighty swings." A jury found Person was acting in self-defense. Gibbons had helped save an innocent man's life, a satisfaction he would savor the rest of his own.

CHAPTER 5
Pancho Villa The Revolutionary

After his season of unemployment, public relations and fund-raising, Gibbons wrangled his way back onto the *Tribune*, where his absence had made folks think kindlier of him and his skills. Indeed, in the fall of 1914, the publishers plucked him from the staff for a prestige assignment. He was to cover the mobilization of American troops near the border between Texas and Mexico. Civil war had broken out between factions led by Mexican generals and was threatening to spill into the U.S.

National security was a preoccupation for the *Tribune's* owners, Robert McCormick and Joseph Patterson, both officers in the Illinois National Guard. McCormick and Patterson saw entangling American soldiers in the border rumpus as a way to assess the army's readiness for action in Europe, where a genuine war had begun that August.

McCormick and Patterson saw American isolationism and pacifism towards Europe as dangerously naïve, and thought Gibbons bright and aggressive enough to rally the *Tribune*'s readers to the interventionist cause.

The Mexican Revolution began in 1910 when the 35-year-long regime of President Porfirio Diaz was challenged by candidate Francisco Modero. Diaz fraudulently won the election. Modero supporters took up arms and what began as a revolt against Diaz eventually turned into a civil war among competing generals that lasted until 1920.

Near Naco, Ariz., Gibbons covered his first battle—Mexicans battling Mexicans—watching the battle with troops from one faction. In his front page Dec., 26, 1914, article, he wrote, "The battle's spectators were frequently interrupted by a bullet singing overhead or splintering wooden siding of the cars."

While in Juarez, Mexico, Gibbons met Hipolito Villa, brother of General Pancho Villa, known for shooting anyone—man, woman or child—he perceived as a foe, putting their backs to their adobe huts and bullets into their hearts. Villa was also known as a man hard to find, forever escaping and earning the nickname, La Cucaracha—the cockroach. Hipolito agreed to take Gibbons to see his hidden brother. Pancho Villa was illiterate and as mercurial as he was ruthless, but on one point he would not waiver. He hated gringos. Especially gringos with notebooks and questions like one who once had talked with him and then written poisonously about him. When an aide read the story to him aloud, Villa swore he would kill the next American journalist he saw.

As he had at Cameron Dam, wheedling his way into the Dietz camp, and at the Minneapolis hotel fire, racing into the flames to snag the registration book, Gibbons took risk to be part of the thrill of being a reporter. When Villa met Gibbons, his rage could not withstand the impression of the charming journalist any more than the Jesuits at Gonzaga, the editors at the *Tribune* and Army Lieutenant George Patton, another fellow with a taste for danger and fame.

Patton, who also had just arrived in Mexico, wrote his wife about what she ought to believe about the battles there: "The *Chicago Tribune* has the only accurate stuff in it by Gibbons." No record exists that the future General Patton and Gibbons met, but the duo did share an admiration for firearms, particularly .45-calibre ivory-handled Colt revolvers. That was the type of sidearm Gibbons, who fancied himself a cowboy, was carrying when he and Villa met at Hipolito's urging. Villa scoffed at the fancy six-gun and told the gringo reporter to get a decent pistola.

Though he disdained Gibbons' weapon, Villa invited the young American to join the 30,000 cavalrymen he was leading into battle with his faction's foes. The prospect enthralled Gibbons, but as a city slicker he was anything but ready for the ride. He learned his first lessons on the trail from saddle sores, wind and sunburn, blisters and chapped skin. But he stayed in the saddle and on the beat, writing story after story of galloping with the romantic madman. His editors and his readers loved it.

Pancho Villa, the Mexican Revolutionary general, whose forces helped overthrow the Mexican president in 1914. Gibbons boldly attached himself to Villa's army and rode with him for four months, thrilling his Chicago Tribune *readers with the flamboyant leader's exploits. Villa was so brazen he attacked U.S. territory in Columbus, N. M., and President Woodrow Wilson sent Army troops to find Villa when he fled back to Mexico. The Army, led by General John Pershing, used trucks and airplanes for the first time but failed to track down the revolutionary.*

After two days' ride, Villa halted his army. One of his lieutenants approached Gibbons. "I think the old man has found what he's after," the man whispered.

The troops had come to a town with a small square. "A bugle sounded," Gibbons wrote. "Quirts hummed through the air, spurs jangled, bugles took up the call up and down the line. Everyone yelled. The exhausted animals caught the fever and plunged. The charge was on."

"As far as I could find out, no one near our position on the line had any idea what was being charged. I am sure I didn't. But apparently it was up ahead somewhere and that was the direction we pressed."

As the fighting began and grew in intensity, Gibbons' horse balked. The animal backed through a door into a house, nearly crushing its terrified occupants –at the same time taking its rider out of fire in what Gibbons called "the best maneuver of the battle."

When he wasn't on horseback, Gibbons cadged transportation usually reserved for robber barons.

Villa had captured train yards and converted a few rail cars into a traveling headquarters with bordello. He decided to bestow a car on Gibbons, who the vain Mexican had come to consider his personal historian. Villa had the rail car professionally painted to read *La Tribuna Chicago—Enviada Especial* (*Chicago Tribune* Special Correspondent). It's not hard to imagine that the showman in Gibbons may have pushed the idea, much to the delight of his publishers in Chicago. Gibbons was living larger than life. He was the only reporter riding with the General. Gibbons could chronicle the General's battles, military and otherwise, as well as his peccadilloes "Next to Villa's sleeping quarters in his private car was an area occupied by three small beds with canopies of pink mosquito netting. The compartment was called 'the chicken coop,' Gibbons wrote. "Youth and beauty were the qualifications of its occupants, who changed frequently. Villa had some of the characteristics of a Sultan."

Gibbons spent about four months with the Cockroach and it was while living in a captured brewery that he witnessed the executions

Gibbons, on top step, endeared himself to Villa, who often traveled by commandeered train car. Villa gave Gibbons the use of a car for his office; it carried a Tribune logo in Spanish.

staged daily of Villa's opponents. Each morning a new group would be lined up and shot. When the war began to go against Villa, Gibbons got out while the getting was good. He convinced Villa to let him take a train north to obtain supplies, a ruse that enabled him to quit Villa's camp.

Later, the U.S. helped Villa's opponent, Gen. Venustino Carranza, rescue a small garrison that Villa's men were besieging. This so enraged the general that on March 9, 1916, he led troops into tiny Columbus, N. M. In retribution, on March 15, General John Pershing led some 10,000 horse soldiers and other troops across the border to capture the Cockroach. Gibbons accompanied Pershing on the hunt for his former protector, filing dispatch upon dispatch. As he had with Villa, Gibbons made a friend of "Black Jack" Pershing, who in years to come would prove a valuable ally, and who in Mexico was the subject of a flattering Gibbons profile that invoked Pershing's "brilliant record" and declared, "There is perhaps no man as skillful in guerilla warfare and Indian fighting."

The same Mexican expedition that earned Gibbons Pershing's friendship proved that National Guard units were not entirely combat-ready. Gibbons wrote in the *Tribune* of the trouble the units had simply getting to Mexico—food shortages, no sleeping cars and other issues. Once there, troops faced brutal heat, relentless insects, grinding work, and boredom. Gibbons wrote about machine gun units with neither machine guns nor bullets, cavalry units lacking horseshoes, infantrymen who had never fired a round and even missing payroll and voucher forms. Sanitation, he said, was a disaster. The expeditionary force did not have enough gasoline to burn its garbage or soldiers' bodily waste. The army had sent them out without lumber, so they could not build the sleeping platforms to keep them out of the quagmire that the rainy season brought.

"I heard Texans of long experience say they would mutiny if forced to such extremes," Gibbons said. "Of course there was no mutiny. The men stood the gaff. They stood it like good fellows. Certainly it was hot. They became dizzy from the sun. Climatic combinations tended to debilitate, to tap strength and stamina, but they bore it. Unaccustomed to the work, unaccustomed to the climate, unaccustomed to the diet, they went at whatever was put before them with blind faith in the belief that it

A pistol-packing Gibbons with General John "Black Jack" Pershing during the Mexican Revolution. The two developed deep mutual respect in Mexico and later during World War I, when Pershing headed the American forces. Wrote Pershing in a letter: "You have always played the game squarely and with courage and I wish to thank you."

was making soldiers of them. Every man in the national guard wanted to be a soldier."

Empathy for the working man was a standard tool of any reporter who knew which hands to stroke and which to bite to stay on a good beat. Gibbons' reporting on the pluck of the little guy in Mexico became a favorite theme. His exposes of army problems so pleased *Tribune* publishers McCormick and Patterson that they published them separately in a special edition as the U.S. edged nearer to involvement in the Great War.

"The proximity of the War in Germany makes military training the greatest question before the nation," the special edition's introduction said. "In a country where the army does not and cannot rule, the public must supply the will for adequate methods."

Gibbons' absence in Mexico provided for a revolution in his home as well. The impetuous Isabella, feeling lonely, struck up a relationship with one John. C. Coulter, whom she had met while with friends at a dance at the Chicago Athletic Club. Further dance dates ensued and she told Gibbons years later in a marital post mortem missive that she had never dreamed that the man had designs on anything but the ballroom arts. But he did, and "it was like a flame in feathers, dear," she wrote.

CHAPTER 6
The Sinking of the Laconia

Americans of late 1916 and early 1917 adamantly disdained the Great War. They had just elected President Woodrow Wilson to a second term on the basis of the slogan, "He Kept Us Out of War!" The carnage in Europe was what many of this nation of immigrants had purposely left their homelands to avoid. Many Americans with roots in Germany—no other country could claim more American descendants—feared becoming scapegoats if the U.S. allied with the British and French. Wilson tried to be true to his sloganeering, but in February 1917, Germany, trying to starve England into submission, resumed unlimited submarine warfare in the Atlantic. Wilson, out of options, broke diplomatic ties with the Kaiser and told German Ambassador Johann Von Bernstorff to leave Washington posthaste. But the president waved no battle flag, instead declaring he would await a German casus belli, or "reason for war."

To return home, Von Bernstorff and staff booked passage on the Danish liner *Frederick VIII*, sailing from New York on Sunday, Feb. 17. *Chicago Tribune* publishers McCormick and Patterson wanted Gibbons, their new London bureau chief and head war correspondent, to sail on the *Frederick VIII* also. The magnates weren't just interested in what the departing German diploma had to say. They wanted Gibbons, fresh from reporting on the Mexican Revolution and our military shortcomings, to survive the journey. The *Frederick VIII* would be sailing with guarantees the vessel would cross the Atlantic in peace, the last boat assured safe passage before the Kriegsmarine set its wolfpacks free to sink allied ships.

From the start of the hostilities in 1914, U-boats—from the German *Unterseeboote*, meaning submarine—had hunted in packs like their namesakes, sending myriad tons of cargo destined for England and France to the bottom. The May, 7 1915 sinking by German torpedo of the *RMS Lusitania*, killing 1,924, including 128 Americans, had caused such outrage that the Reich called in its undersea captains and crews. Seeds for U.S. war

RMS Laconia, *a Cunard passenger liner, sunk by German submarine U-50 off the coast of Ireland on Feb. 25, 1917, with Gibbons aboard. He declined passage on a safe ship carrying the German ambassador, specifically choosing the* Laconia *because he thought it would be sunk. Rescued in a packed row boat, Gibbons wrote a 4,000-word news story seen to this day as one of the greatest examples of deadline reporting ever produced. Gibbons' story was accurate right down to the Chicago angle and a second-hand contemporaneous interview with the U-boat commander who sank the ship. His article was read in the White House and read aloud in both Houses of Congress. Within weeks, the United States had joined allies in war against Germany. The* Laconia *is often confused with the* RMS Lusitania, *sunk two years earlier by Germany, killing 128 Americans, and planting the seeds for war.*

entry had been planted then, and now the wolfpacks would be unleashed once again.

Tribune management pulled some strings and paid a heavy premium far above the going first-class $52 rate to put Gibbons on the *Frederick*. But he refused the ticket. Gibbons "was having none of this namby-pamby nonsense," wrote David Randall in *The Great Reporters*. "He found out which would be the first boat out of New York to defy the German ultimatum and, in the hope of a sensational scoop, booked himself on it. The ship was Cunard's *Laconia* and when on 17 February, it left New York, there in stateroom B-19 was Gibbons, perhaps the only man ever to sail the Atlantic hoping that his ship would be sunk."

Across the cold Atlantic, the outwardly serene but inwardly anxious Gibbons anticipated the story of a lifetime—and he got it. His story from Ireland is reprinted entirely here.

"Queenstown, February 26, 1917.

I have serious doubts whether this is a real story. I am not entirely certain that it is not all a dream. I feel that in a few minutes I may wake up back in stateroom B-19 on the promenade deck of the Cunard Laconia and hear my cockney steward informing me with an abundance of "and sirs" that it is a fine morning.

It is now a little over thirty hours since I stood on the slanting decks of the big liner, listened to the lowering of the lifeboats, and heard the hiss of escaping steam and the roar of ascending rockets as they tore lurid rents in the black sky and cast their red glare over the roaring sea.

I am writing this within thirty minutes after stepping on the dock here in Queenstown from the British mine sweeper which picked up our open lifeboat after an eventful six hours of drifting and darkness and bailing and pulling on the oars and of straining aching eyes toward that empty, meaningless horizon in search of help.

But dream or fact, here it is:

The Cunard liner Laconia, 18,000 tons burden, carrying seventy-three passengers—men, women, and children—of whom six were American citizens—manned by a mixed crew of two hundred and sixteen, bound from New York to Liverpool, and loaded with foodstuffs, cotton, and war material, was torpedoed without warning by a German submarine last night off the Irish coast. The vessel sank in about forty minutes.

Two American citizens, mother and daughter, listed from Chicago, and former residents there, are among the dead. They were Mrs. Mary E. Hoy and Miss Elizabeth Hoy. I have talked with a seaman who was in the same lifeboat with the two Chicago women and he has told me that he saw their lifeless bodies washing out of the sinking lifeboat. The American survivors are Mrs. F. E. Harris, of Philadelphia, who was the last woman to leave the Laconia; the Rev. Father Wareing, of St. Joseph's Seminary, Baltimore; Arthur T. Kirby, of New York, and myself.

A former Chicago woman, now the wife of a British subject, was among the survivors. She is Mrs. Henry George Boston, the daughter of Granger Farwell, of Lake Forest.

After leaving New York, passengers and crew had had three drills with the lifeboats. All were supplied with lifebelts and assigned to places in the twelve big lifeboats poised over the side from the davits of the top deck.

Submarines had been a chief part of the conversation during the entire trip, but the subject had been treated lightly, although all ordered precautions were strictly in force. After the first explanatory drill on the second day out from New York, from which we sailed on Saturday, February 17, the 'abandon ship' signal—five quick blasts on the whistle—had summoned us twice to our lifebelts and heavy wraps, among which I included a flask and a flashlight, and to a roll call in front of our assigned boats on the top deck.

On Sunday we knew generally we were in the danger zone, though we did not know definitely where we were—or at least the passengers did not. In the afternoon during a short chat with Captain W. R. D. Irvine, the ship's commander, I had mentioned that I would like to see a chart and note our position on the ocean. He replied: "Oh, would you?" with a smiling, rising inflection that meant, "It is jolly well none of your business."

Prior to this my cheery early-morning steward had told us that we would make Liverpool by Monday night and I used this information in another question to the captain.

"When do we land?" I asked.

"I don't know," replied Capt. Irvine, but my steward told me later it would be Tuesday after dinner.

The first cabin passengers were gathered in the lounge Sunday evening, with the exception of the bridge fiends in the smoke-room.

"Poor Butterfly" was dying wearily on the talking machine and several couples were dancing.

About the tables in the smoke-room the conversation was limited to the announcement of bids and orders to the stewards. Before the fireplace was a little gathering which had been dubbed as the Hyde Park corner—an allusion I don't quite fully understand. This group had about exhausted available discussion when I projected a new bone of contention.

"What do you say are our chances of being torpedoed?" I asked.

"Well," drawled the deliberative Mr. Henry Chetham, a London solicitor, "I should say four thousand to one."

Lucien J. Jerome, of the British diplomatic service, returning with an Ecuadorian valet from South America, interjected: "Considering the zone and the class of this ship, I should put it down at two hundred and fifty to one that we don't meet a sub." At this moment the ship gave a sudden lurch sideways and forward. There was a muffled noise like the slamming of some large door at a good distance away. The slightness of the shock and the meekness of the report compared with my imagination were disappointing. Every man in the room was on his feet in an instant.

"We're hit!" shouted Mr. Chetham.

"That's what we've been waiting for," said Mr. Jerome.

"What a lousy torpedo!" said Mr. Kirby in typical New Yorkese. "It must have been a fizzer."

I looked at my watch. It was 10:30 P.M.

Then came the five blasts on the whistle. We rushed down the corridor leading from the smoke-room at the stern to the lounge, which was amidships. We were running, but there was no panic. The occupants of the lounge were just leaving by the forward doors as we entered.

It was dark on the landing leading down to the promenade deck, where the first-class staterooms were located. My pocket flashlight, built like a fountain pen, came in handy on the landing.

We reached the promenade deck. I rushed into my stateroom, B-19, grabbed my overcoat and the water bottle and special life-preserver with which the *Tribune* had equipped me before sailing. Then I made my way to the upper deck on that same dark landing.

I saw the chief steward opening an electric switch box in the wall and turning on the switch. Instantly the boat decks were illuminated. That illumination saved lives.

The torpedo had hit us well astern on the starboard side and had missed the engines and the dynamos. I had not noticed the deck lights before. Throughout the voyage our decks had remained dark at night and all cabin portholes were clamped down and all windows covered with opaque paint.

The illumination of the upper deck on which I stood made the darkness of the water sixty feet below appear all the blacker when I peered over the edge at my station, boat No. 10.

Already the boat was loading up and men were busy with the ropes. I started to help near a davit that seemed to be giving trouble, but I was stoutly ordered to get out of the way and get into the boat.

We were on the port side, practically opposite the engine well. Up and down the deck passengers and crew were donning lifebelts, throwing on overcoats, and taking positions in the boats. There were a number of women, but only one appeared hysterical—little Miss Titsie Siklosi, a French-Polish actress, who was being cared for by her manager, Cedric P. Ivatt, appearing on the passenger list as from New York.

Steam began to hiss somewhere from the giant gray funnels that towered above. Suddenly there was a roaring swish as a rocket soared upward from the captain's bridge, leaving a comet's tail of fire. I watched it as it described a graceful arc in the black void overhead, and then, with an audible pop, it burst into a flare of brilliant white light.

There was a tilt to the deck. It was listing to starboard at just the angle that would make it necessary to reach for support to enable one to stand upright. In the meantime electric floodlights—large white enameled funnels containing clusters of bulbs—had been suspended from the promenade deck and illuminated the dark water that rose and fell on the slanting side of the ship.

"Lower away!" Someone gave the order and we started down with a jerk towards the seemingly hungry rising and falling swells.

Then we stopped with another jerk and remained suspended in mid-air while the man at the bow and the stern swore and tussled with the lowering ropes. The stern of the lifeboat was down, the bow up, leaving us at an angle of about forty-five degrees. We clung to the seats to save ourselves from falling out.

"Who's got a knife, a knife, a knife!" shouted a sweating seaman in the bow. "Great God, give him a knife!" bawled a half-dressed, jibbering Negro stoker, who wrung his hands in the stern.

A hatchet was thrust into my hand and I forwarded it to the bow. There was a flash of sparks as it crashed down on the holding pulley. One strand of rope parted and down plunged the bow, too quick for the stern man. We came to a jerky stop with the stern in the air and the bow down, but the stern managed to lower away until the dangerous angle was eliminated.

The Chicago Daily Tribune.

THE WORLD'S GREATEST NEWSPAPER

FINAL EDITION

VOLUME LXXVI.—NO. 51. C.   WEDNESDAY, FEBRUARY 28, 1917.—TWENTY-FOUR PAGES.   ★ ★ PRICE ONE CENT.

HOW LACONIA SANK

WILSON RULES CASE OF LINER IS 'OVERT ACT'

ALD. MERRIAM AND BUCK LOSE AT PRIMARIES

Werner and Kearns Also Beaten—School Issue a Big Factor.

FULL POWERS WILL BE GIVEN TO PRESIDENT

Senate Bill Makes It Mandatory on Him to Arm Ships.

LATE NEWS BULLETINS

FLOYD GIBBONS CABLES FIRST COMPLETE STORY OF LINER TORPEDOING

Concert and Dancing Changes to Rush to Life Craft; Heroism and Discipline Save Many of Passengers.

BY FLOYD P. GIBBONS.

WONDER IF IT AIN'T PURTY NEAR TIME TO BEGIN TO LOAD HER UP?

THE NOMINEES

THE WEATHER

ON THE LACONIA

Then both tried to lower together. The list of the ship's side became greater, but, instead of our boat sliding down it like a toboggan, the taffrail caught and was held. As the lowering continued, the other side dropped down and we found ourselves clinging on at a new angle and looking straight down on the water.

A hand slipped into mine and a voice sounded huskily close to my ear. It was the little old German-Jew traveling man who was disliked in the smoke-room because he used to speak too certainly of things he was uncertain of and whose slightly Teutonic dialect made him as popular as smallpox with the British passengers.

"My boy, I can't see nutting," he said. "My glasses slipped and I am falling. Hold me, please."

I managed to reach out and join hands with another man on the other side of the old man and together we held him in. He hung heavily over our arms, grotesquely grasping all he had saved from his stateroom—a gold headed cane and an extra hat.

Many hands and feet pushed the boat from the side of the ship and we sagged down again, this time smacking squarely on the pillowy top of a rising swell. It felt more solid than midair, at least. But we were far from being off. The pulleys twice stuck in their fastenings, bow and stern, and the one axe passed forward and back, and with it my flashlight, as the entangling ropes that held us to the sinking Laconia were cut away.

Some shout from that confusion of sound caused me to look up and I really did so with the fear that one of the nearby boats was being lowered upon us.

A man was jumping, as I presumed, with the intention of landing in the boat and I prepared to avoid the impact, but he passed beyond us and plunged into the water three feet from the edge of the boat. He bobbed to the surface immediately.

"It's Duggan!" shouted a man next to me.

I flashed the light on the ruddy, smiling face and water-plastered hair of the little Canadian, our fellow saloon passenger. We pulled him over the side. He sputtered out a mouthful of water and the first words he said were:

"I wonder if there is anything to that lighting three cigarettes off the same match? I was up above trying to loosen the rope to this boat. I loosened it and then got tangled up in it. The boat went down, but I was jerked up. I jumped for it."

His first reference concerned our deliberate tempting of fates early in the day when he, Kirby, and I lighted three cigarettes from the same match and Duggan told us that he had done the same thing many a time.

As we pulled away from the side of the ship, its ranking and receding terrace of lights stretched upward. The ship was slowly turning over. We were opposite that part occupied by the engine room. There was a tangle of oars, spars, and rigging on the seat and considerable confusion before four of the big sweeps could be manned on either side of the boat.

The jibbering, bullet-headed Negro was pulling directly behind me and I turned to quiet him as his frantic reaches with his oar were hitting me in the back. In the dull light from the upper decks I looked into his slanting face, eyes all whites and lips moving convulsively. Besides being frightened, the man was freezing in the thin cotton shirt that composed his entire upper covering. He would work feverishly to get warm.

"Get away from her; get away from her," he kept repeating. "When the water hits her hot boilers, she'll blow up, and there are just tons and tons of shrapnel in the hold!"

His excitement spread to other members of the crew in the boat. The ship's baker, designated by his pantry headgear, became a competing alarmist, and a white fireman, whose blasphemy was nothing short of profound, added to the confusion by cursing everyone.

It was the give-way of nerve tension. It was bedlam and nightmare.

Seeking to establish some authority in our boat, I made my way to the stern and there found an old, white-haired sea captain, a second-cabin passenger, with whom I had talked before. He was bound from Nova Scotia with codfish. His sailing schooner, the Secret, had broken in two, but he and his crew had been taken off by a tramp and taken back to New York. He had sailed from there on the Ryndam, which, after almost crossing the Atlantic, had turned back. The Laconia was his third attempt to get home. His name is Captain Dear.

"The rudder's gone, but I can steer with an oar," he said. "I will take charge, but my voice is gone. You'll have to shout the orders."

There was only one way to get the attention of the crew and that was by an overpowering blast of profanity. I did my best and was rewarded by silence while I made the announcement that in the absence of the ship's officer assigned to the boat, Captain Dear would take charge. There was no dissent and under the captain's orders the boat's head was held to the wind to prevent us from being swamped by the increasing swells.

We rested on our oars, with all eyes turned on the still-lighted Laconia. The torpedo had struck at 10:30 P.M. According to our ship's time, it was thirty minutes after that hour that another dull thud, which was accompanied by a noticeable drop in the hulk, told its story of the second torpedo that the submarine had dispatched through the engine room and the boat's vitals from a distance of 200 yards.

We watched silently during the next minute, as the tiers of lights dimmed slowly from white to yellow, then to red, and nothing was left but the murky mourning of the night, which hung over all like a pall.

A mean, cheese-colored crescent of a moon revealed one horn above a rag bundle of clouds low in the distance. A rim of blackness settled around our little world, relieved only by general leering stars in the zenith, and where the Laconia lights had shone there remained only the dim outline of a blacker hulk standing out above the water like a jagged headland, silhouetted against the overcast sky.

The ship sank rapidly at the stern until at last its nose stood straight in the air. Then it slid silently down and out of sight like a piece of disappearing scenery in a panorama spectacle.

Boat No. 3 stood closest to the ship and rocked about in a perilous sea of clashing spars and wreckage. As the boat's crew steadied its head into the wind, a black hulk, glistening wet and standing about eight feet above the surface of the water, approached slowly and came to a stop opposite the boat and not six feet from the side of it.

"Vot ship was dot?" the correct words in throaty English with the German accent came from the dark hulk, according to Chief Steward Ballyn's statement to me later.

"The Laconia," Ballyn answered.

"Vot?"

"The Laconia, Cunard line," responded the steward.

"Vot did she veigh?" was the next question from the submarine.

"Eighteen thousand tons."

"Any passengers?"

"Seventy-three," replied Ballyn, "men, women, and children, some of them in this boat. She had over two hundred in the crew."

"Did she carry cargo?"

"Yes."

"Vell, you'll be all right. The patrol will pick you up soon," and without further sound, save for the almost silent fixing of the conning tower lid, the submarine moved off.

"I thought it best to make my answers truthful and satisfactory, sir," said Ballyn when he repeated the conversation to me word for word. "I was thinking of the women and children in the boat. I feared every minute that somebody in our boat might make a hostile move, fire a revolver, or throw something at the submarine. I feared the consequences of such an act."

There was no assurance of an early pickup, even though the promise was from a German source, for the rest of the boats, whose occupants—if they felt and spoke like those in my boat—were more than mildly anxious about our plight and the prospects of rescue.

We made preparations for the siege with the elements. The weather was a great factor. That black rim of clouds looked ominous. There was a good promise of rain. February has a reputation for nasty weather in the north Atlantic. The wind was cold and seemed to be rising. Our boat bobbed about like a cork on the swells, which fortunately were not choppy.

How much rougher weather could the boat stand? This question and the conditions were debated pro and con.

Had our rockets been seen? Did the first torpedo put the wireless out of business? Did anybody hear our S.O.S.? Was there enough food and drinking water in the boat to last? That brought us to an inventory of our small craft, and after much difficulty we found a lamp, a can of powder flares, a tin of ship's biscuits, matches, and spare oil.

The lamp was lighted. Other lights were visible at small distances every time we mounted the crest of the swells. The boats remained quite close together at first. One boat came within sound and I recognized the Harry-Lauder-like voice of the second assistant purser, last heard on Wednesday at the ship's concert. There was singing, "I Want to Marry 'Arry," and "I Love to Be a Sailor."

Mrs. Boston was in that boat with her husband. She told me later that an attempt had been made to sing "Tipperary" and "Rule, Britannia," but the thought of that slinking dark hull of destruction that might have been a part of the immediate darkness resulted in an abandonment of the effort.

"Who's the officer in that boat?" came a cheery hail from a nearby light.

"What the hell is it to you?" bawled out our half-frozen Negro, for no reason imaginable other than, possibly, the relief of his feelings.

"Brain him with a pin, somebody!" yelled our profound oaths man, and accompanied the order with a warmth of language that must have relieved the Negro's chill.

The fear of some of the boats crashing together produced a general inclination toward further separation on the part of all the little units of survivors, with the result that soon the small craft stretched out for several miles, all of them endeavoring to keep their heads into the wind.

And then we saw the first light, the first sign of help coming, the first searching glow of white brilliance, deep down on the somber sides of the black pot of night that hung over us. I don't know what direction that came from—none of us knew north from south—there was nothing but water and sky. But the light—it just came from over there where we pointed.

We nudged violently sick boat-mates and directed their gaze and aroused them to an appreciation of the sight that gave us new life.

It was over there—first a trembling quiver of silver against the blackness, then, drawing closer, it defined itself as a beckoning finger, although still too far away to see our feeble efforts to attract.

We nevertheless wasted valuable flares and the ship's baker, self-ordained custodian of biscuit tin, did the honors handsomely to the extent of a biscuit apiece to each of the twenty-three occupants in the boat.

"Pull starboard, sonnies," sang out old Captain Dear, his gray chin whiskers literally bristling with joy in the light of the round lantern which he held aloft.

We pulled lustily, forgetting the strain and pain of innards torn and racked from vain vomiting, oblivious of blistered hands and yet half-frozen feet.

Then a nodding of that finger of light—a happy, snapping, crapshooting finger that seemed to say "Come on, you men," like a dice player wooing the bones—led us to believe that our lights had been seen. This was the fact, for immediately the coming vessel flashed on its green and red sidelights and we saw it was headed for our position.

We floated off its stern for a while as it maneuvered for the best position in which it could take us on with the sea that was running higher and higher, it seemed to me.

"Come alongside port!" was megaphoned to us, and as fast as we could we swung under the stern and felt our way broadside toward the ship's side. A dozen flashlights blinked down to us and orders began to flow fast and thick.

When I look back on the night, I don't know which was the more hazardous—our descent from the Laconia or our ascent to our rescuer. One minute the swell lifted us almost level with the rail of the low-built patrol boat and mine sweeper; the next receding wave would carry us down into a gulf over which the ship's side glowed like a slimy, dripping cliff. A score of hands reached out, and we were suspended in the husky, tattooed arms of those doughty British jack tars, looking up into the weather-beaten, youthful faces, mumbling thanks and thankfulness, and reading in the gold lettering on their pancake hats the legend "H.M.S. Laburnum."

The Washington Times

WASHINGTON, WEDNESDAY EVENING, FEBRUARY 28, 1917.

FORECAST:
now Tonight
rt on Page Two.)

10,090.

AGREE UNTIL MARCH 5

ke During In-
spelled By
ficials.

ASSISTANCE

t Over Reports
ithin Forty-
ours.

WASHINGTON MAN DESCRIBES SINKING OF LINER LACONIA

Muffled Blow and Lurch Only Warning, Says
Floyd P. Gibbons In Graphic Story
of Horrors of Disaster.

By FLOYD P. GIBBONS.
(Copyright, 1917, by the Chicago Tribune.)

QUEENSTOWN, Feb. 26 (via London, Feb. 27).—I have
serious doubts whether this is a real story. I am not entirely
certain that it is not all a dream and that in a few minutes I
will wake up back in stateroom B 19 on the promenade deck of
the Cunarder Laconia and hear my cockney steward informing
me with an abundance of "and sirs" that it is a fine morning.

It is now a little over thirty hours since I stood on the
slanting decks of the big liner, listened to the lowering of the
lifeboats, heard the hiss of escaping steam and the roar of ascending rockets as they tore lurid rents in the black sky and cast
their red glare over the roaring sea.

THIRTY MINUTES AFTER BEING SAVED.

I am writing this within thirty
minutes after stepping on the deck
here in Queenstown from the British
mine sweeper which picked up our
open lifeboat after an eventful six
hours of drifting and darkness and
bailing and pulling on the oars and
of straining aching eyes toward that
empty, meaningless horizon in search
of help. Dat, dream, or fact, here
it is

The Cunard liner Laconia 18,000
tons burden, carrying seventy-three
passengers, men, women and children, of whom six were American
citizens, manned by a mixed crew of

(Continued on Fourth Page)

CLERKS' RAISE IS THREATENED BY HOKE SMITH

Georgia Senator Announces He
Will Oppose All Appropri-
ation Bills.

HAS SOME STRONG BACKING

Extra Session Looks More Prob-
able Because of New
Trouble.

FILIBUSTER MAY PASSAGE OF A BILL IN PRES

GERARD SAILS TODAY

Former Ambassador Gerard sails today from
Spain, for America, according to a dispatch
that reached the State Department.

He denies that he gave out any interviews to corre
while in Europe despite the fact that he was
great length in the newspapers.

WAR ADVICES SENT PENFIELD

Ambassador Elkus Also In-
structed on What to Do If
Hostilities Come.

POWER LIM BY LAWMA

House Foreign Affai
tee Grants Wilso
quest Only Pi

D. C. GUARDSMEN TO DETRAIN TOMORROW

THE HALF-AND-HALF ABOLISHED IN BILL

O. L. HOUSEL GETS POST

Appointed Assistant Electrical
Engineer for District.

We had been six hours in the open boats, all of which began coming alongside one after another. Wet and bedraggled survivors were lifted aboard. Women and children first was the rule.

The scenes of reunion were heart-gripping. Men who had remained strangers to one another aboard the Laconia wrung each other by the hand, or embraced without shame the frail little wife of a Canadian chaplain who had found one of her missing children delivered up from another boat. She smothered the child with ravenous mother kisses while tears of joy streamed down her face.

Boat after boat came alongside. The waterlogged craft containing the captain came last. A rousing cheer went up as he landed his feet on the deck, one mangled hand hanging limp at his side.

The jack tars divested themselves of outer clothing and passed the garments over to the shivering members of the Laconia's crew.

The little officers' quarters down under the quarter-deck were turned over to the women and children. Two of the Laconia's stewardesses passed boiling basins of navy cocoa and aided in the disentanglement of wet and matted tresses.

The men grouped themselves near steam pipes in the petty officers' quarters or over the gratings of the engine rooms, where new life was to be had from the upward blasts of heated air that brought with them the smell of bilge water and oil and sulfur from the bowels of the vessel.

The injured—all minor cases, sprained backs, wrenched legs, or mashed hands—were put away in bunks under the care of the ship's doctor.

Dawn was melting the eastern ocean gray to pink when the task was finished.

In the officers' quarters, now invaded by the men, somebody happened to touch a key on the small wooden organ, and this was enough to send some callous seafaring fingers over the keys in a rhythm unquestionably religious and so irresistible under the circumstances that, although no one knew the words, the air was taken up in a serious humming chant by all in the room.

At the last note of the amen, little Father Wareing, his black garb snaggled in places and badly soiled, stood before the center table and lifted his head back until the morning light, filtering through the open hatch above him, shone down on his kindly, weary face. He recited the Lord's Prayer, all present joined, and the simple, impressive service ended as simply as it had begun.

Two minutes later I saw the old German-Jew traveling man limping about on one lame leg with a little boy in his arms, collecting big round British pennies for the youngster.

A survey and cruise of the nearby area revealed no more occupied boats and the mine sweeper, with its load of survivors numbering 267, steamed away to the east. A half an hour's steaming and the vessel stopped within hailing distance of two sister ships, towards one of which an open boat, manned by jackies, was pulling.

I saw the hysterical French-Polish actress, her hair wet and bedraggled, lifted out of the boat and handed up the companionway. Then a little boy, his fresh pink face and golden hair shining in the morning light, was passed upward, followed by some other survivors, numbering fourteen in all, who had been found half drowned and almost dead from exposure in a partially wrecked boat that was just sinking.

This was the boat in which Mrs. Hoy and her daughter lost their lives and in which Cedric P. Ivatt of New York, who was the manager for the actress, died. It has not been ascertained here whether Mr. Ivatt was an American or a British subject.

One of the survivors of this boat was Able Seaman Walley, who was transferred to the Laburnum.

"Our boat—No. 8—was smashed in lowering," he said. "I was in the bow, Mrs. Hoy and her daughter were sitting toward the stern. The boat filled with water rapidly. It was no use trying to bail it out—there was a big hole in the side and it came in too fast. It just sunk to the water's edge and only stayed up on account of the tanks in it. It was completely awash. Every swell rode clear over us and we had to hold our breath until we came to the surface again. The cold water just takes the strength out of you.

"The women got weaker and weaker, then a wave came and washed both of them out of the boat. There were lifebelts on their bodies and they floated away, but I believe they were dead before they were washed overboard." With such stories singing in our ears, with exchanges of experiences pathetic and humorous, we came steaming into Queenstown harbor shortly after ten o'clock tonight. We pulled up at a dock lined with waiting ambulances and khaki-clad men, who directed the survivors to the various hotels about the town, where they are being quartered.

The question being asked of the Americans on all sides is: "Is it the casus belli?"

American Consul Wesley Frost is forwarding all information to Washington with a speed and carefulness

resulting from the experiences in handling twenty-five previous submarine disasters in which the United States has had an interest, especially in the survivors landed at this port.

His best figures on the Laconia sinking are: total survivors landed here, 267; landed at Bantry, 14; total on board, 294; missing, 13.

The latest information from Bantry, the only other port at which survivors were known to have landed, confirms the report of the death of Mrs. Hoy and her daughter."

Gibbons had risked it all for a scoop, and the wager paid off beyond measure, with what may be the greatest piece of wartime reporting ever. He lived the story, and then, under horrific conditions and at a myth-making pace, batted out a piece detailed right down to the hometown angle, the irony of his fellow passengers speculating on the odds of being hit and the seemingly unprecedented accomplishment of a nearly contemporaneous indirect interview with the U-boat captain who sank them.

More important than technique, timing and style, Gibbons, with his first-person account of the *Laconia* sinking, helped change Americans' isolationist minds. As readers encountered his reporting in the Midwest and then across the country, the skill that had made Gibbons the apple of the *Tribune*'s eye moved people. Senators and Representatives angrily read the piece word-for-word into the record from their floors. Within five weeks, amid revelations that Germany had been trying in secret to enlist Mexico and Japan against America and the Allies, the United States declared that a state of war existed with Germany. Woodrow Wilson had gotten his casus belli because Floyd Gibbons had gotten his story—again.

CHAPTER 7
With the Troops in Europe

Gibbons' *Laconia* reporting made him the wunderkind at the *Trib* and a journalistic sensation worldwide. Every reporter and editor of the day marveled at the dispatch he had filed under extreme duress and with complete accuracy.

Gibbons happily embraced the acclaim with bravado and a shrewd boldness that would earn ever greater renown. When General John J. "Black Jack" Pershing, commander of the American Expeditionary Force, slipped into England on June 8, 1917, aboard the White Star liner *Baltic*, British censors barred reporters from naming the port. Gibbons end-ran the embargo with the clever squib: "Pershing landed today at an English port and was given a hearty welcome by the Mayor of Liverpool." He had been a scamp and a scalawag at Georgetown, in the Wisconsin backwoods, and at cop shops in Minneapolis and Chicago--and now he was at it on the international stage.

Prankishness aside, Gibbons brought to his coverage a high degree of admiration for the military and for Pershing, a congenial source since their days galloping together in Mexico, and whose brass he was not above polishing.

"Pershing and his staff stepped ashore. Lean, clean, keen—those are the words that described their appearance," Gibbons wrote. "That was the way they impressed their critical [British] brothers in arms." The polishing paid off that first week in Europe when military authorities gave Gibbons hand-signed permission to personally accompany Pershing across the English Channel to France. Gibbons' wife followed not long after to serve as his secretary in the Paris *Trib* office.

On the Channel crossing, it struck Gibbons that U-boats seemed not to concern Pershing a whit. "I don't believe the General ever gave them so much as a thought," the newsman wrote. But submarines concerned Gibbons. He knew the term "torpedoed" as more than a metaphor. His *Tribune* copy that day notes reassuringly that as Pershing sailed from Folkstone, England, to Boulogne, France, he did so under a protective canopy of dirigibles, warplanes and vessels armed for combat.

From Boulogne, Pershing and his party, including Gibbons, rode a private train to Paris, where the AEF commander broke from war planning to go to the Picpus Cemetery to visit the tomb of Gilbert du Motier, known to Americans as the Marquis de Lafayette, hero of the Revolution.

The American delegation chose July 4, 1917, to lay a wreath on Lafayette's tomb and General Pershing was said to declare dramatically: "Lafayette, we are here." Gibbons and other reporters attributed the quote to the General but, in fact, it was Col. Charles Stanton, nephew of Civil War Secretary of War Edward Stanton, who uttered the famous phrase. American censors may have only allowed Pershing to be quoted that day, or perhaps pack reporting prevailed when confusion over who said what arose. In those cases, the pack, sometimes shunted to the side out of hearing or observation, decides as an informal group on such details. One correspondent present that day, Naboth Hedin, insisted 40 years later he was 20 feet from Pershing and heard him say it, but Pershing himself wrote he didn't recall saying "anything so splendid." Gibbons later had a chance to correct the record writing a book on the early days of the war but didn't, an indication no one raised questions of accuracy at the time, or perhaps proof of Gibbons' belief that if Pershing didn't say it, he should have.

If it was pack journalism that did cause the misattribution, then this incident provided further fuel to Gibbons' fiery hate of the phenomenon. He so bristled at being part of a pack that when he reached the front near Nancy, he sought and got permission to embed himself with Battalion A of the Sixth Field Artillery Regiment, First Expeditionary Division. There was brilliant method in his choice. The Sixth was the first Regiment in the Brigade and A was the first battery of the regiment. "I knew that we would march out in that order, that Battery A would entrain first, detrain first, go in line first, and I hoped to be present at the firing of the first

American shot in the war," Gibbons wrote in his war history and memoir, *And They Thought We Wouldn't Fight.* Understanding correctly that remaining with other reporters in the pack would keep him from seeing action as he wanted to experience it, Gibbons vanished into the artilleryman's life.

Colleagues had no idea where Gibbons had gone. For six weeks they waited for the opening shot. Finally word went out that they were going to the front. "As they rolled along, they exchanged the odd tut-tutting that Gibbons—wherever he was—would miss the story," wrote *The Great Reporters'* Randall. "Some of them may have even meant it."

The pack was five miles from the front at Bathelemont in northwestern France when a French sentry halted the journalists to allow a military convoy to pass. The reporters pulled off the road, lit up Gauloises, and watched a U.S. artillery company pass. One reporter looked up "and thought he saw, sitting beside a field gun, a familiar figure," wrote Randall. "Well I'll be damned," he shouted. "There's Gibbons. How the hell did he get there?"

Gibbons was well positioned that day but not perfectly so. Battalion A was outhustled by nearby Battery C, whose men gave up their meals and rest breaks to pull a cannon by hand across muddy fields. They managed to set up their 75 mm gun a mile or so behind allied lines just to be able to claim to have been the first to fire at the enemy target, a group of 150 mm guns behind the German line.

Gibbons ran to the firing gun from his position in plenty of time to take extensive notes of the shot made at five minutes and ten seconds after six on the morning of Oct. 23, 1917. Along with other notes, Gibbons jotted the gunners' names and roles and even snared the empty brass casing from that first round—which years later he would give to one of those artillery men, Sgt. Alex Arch. For some time, it was thought a red-haired soldier had fired the shot and President Wilson had been awarded the empty shell. Gibbons had settled the matter of who fired the first shot when *The New York Times* in 1918 wrote an article on the subject and Gibbons made it clear to the *Times* reporter it was Arch, the "swarthy gunner from South Bend," who held the national distinction.

Arch pulled the cord on the French 75 that day and Gibbons for some years had tried to track him down to give him the shell he saved. But it took until 1931, when he found him at a Studebaker plant in Ft. Wayne, Ind. Showman Gibbons, by then a famous broadcaster, invited him to the Chicago Press Club for the presentation, and the veteran dutifully received it and somehow confirmed it was indeed the first shell.

Gibbons long dined out on both the first shot story and its aftermath. His competitors in the press that day of the first shot howled so long and hard about being scooped by Gibbons that the Army was forced to take some action. The Army arrested Gibbons for being where he supposedly wasn't supposed to be. *The New York Times* reported: "He now holds the order of his arrest as one of his proudest possessions."

CHAPTER 8
The Feeling of Lead

In Washington, D.C., in the 1890s Civil War veterans were a common sight, human reminders of what war could do. No matter what neighborhood, no matter what street, pedestrians eventually would cross paths with a man of years who had fought in the War Between the States, his hair now gray, with an empty sleeve pinned up or hobbling on crutches or making his difficult way in a wheelchair.

Boys of the era, like boys of many eras, would have been immensely curious about those limbs, how they came to be lost, and what it felt like to be wounded. Even amid such grisly reality, boys have always played soldier, acting out the drama of falling to an enemy bullet.

But bullets flew in the capital during peacetime, too, and with fatal result. On August 6, 1894, Gonzaga College began its annual Garden Party, a highlight of Catholic Washington's calendar. Among the events was a shooting exhibition. As the men of the adults-only Emmet Guard were taking target practice behind the school, Edward Russell, 7, who lived nearby at 37 K Street, was watching the riflemen from atop a fence when a stray round killed him. A coroner's jury determined that it was not a drill team member but an unknown youth who had fired the fatal shot. Floyd Gibbons, like Russell, was 7 when the tragedy occurred and rocked the Catholic community. How could he not have wondered how it felt to be shot like Edward Russell?

Years later, as a police reporter in Minneapolis, Milwaukee and Chicago, Gibbons again saw what guns could do. He did his best to translate that experience into words, but success eluded him. "I could never learn from the victim…the precise feeling…as the piece of lead struck," he wrote later.

That "precise feeling" became all too clear in early June 1918. German forces pushed west to within 40 miles of Paris, thanks to 50 additional German divisions being freed by the Russian surrender on the eastern front and being immediately sent west in hopes of defeating the Allies before the Yanks got to the front lines. The French and English could only hold them so long. On Tuesday, June 5, Allied planners inserted the 5th and 6th U.S. Marines and the 9th and 21st U. S. Infantry into the front lines to push back the Hun from a forest in Belleau, a district near the Marne River in Picardy. The Marines held down the left and right flanks near the picturesque village of Lucy-le-Bocage.

French commanders and their English counterparts had considerable anxiety about just how well the green doughboys and leathernecks would do in a now-or-never situation. Gibbons, wearing his Army-issue Press arm band, and Lt. Arthur Hartzell[5], a former *New York Times* reporter, now in army intelligence, caught a ride from Paris that morning to the battle site, 40 miles east. Correspondents were required to have an Army handler and Hartzell was Gibbons'. The two drove along roads clogged with trucks carrying troops and ammunition to battle and the wounded back to the Paris hospitals. Choking road dust that hot June day amplified confusion. It was hard to see and hard to hear as the thump and roar of German artillery got louder with each mile.

Deposited at La Voie du Chatel, the headquarters of Fifth Marine Commander Colonel W.C. Neville, Gibbons turned over to his *Trib* driver a news dispatch to be delivered to the censors in Paris. "I am up at the front and entering Belleau Wood with the U.S. Marines," it read. He included an account of the battle he expected to cover and then correct and flesh out when he returned that afternoon.

Hartzell and Gibbons met with Neville. The *Tribune* reporter said he wanted to see the fighting. Neville strongly discouraged the men, telling them it's "damned hot up there." Gibbons insisted. "Go wherever you like and as far as you like," Neville finally said.

The men headed west from Lucy-le-Bocage with the Third Battalion of the Fifth, encountering flurries of shredded paper—to lighten their packs, the Marines had torn up and discarded letters from home. At

Bataille de la Marne 1918

Environs de CHATEAU-THIERRY — BELLEAU - L'Ecole et le Bois de Belleau
The School and Belleau Woods

Remains of a school at the Battle of Belleau Wood in June 1918. The Germans had pushed to within 40 miles of Paris and were met by U.S. Army and Marine units determined to stop their drive. In 1924 the U.S. Marine Band performed a march entitled Belleau Wood to mark the battle's anniversary. The march was composed by Captain Taylor Branson who became band director in 1927 and sent two sons to Gonzaga, Albert '33 and James '35. Grandson Vincent '68 attended as did great-grandson Kevin '88.

the Marine front line they found the Yanks had set up a machine gun nest. A Hotchkiss 8 was firing at a German nest 200 yards away in a woods separated by a wheat field. As the sides traded bursts of automatic fire, bullets rattled and tore above Gibbons' head.

At five minutes before 5 p.m., word came that the Marines were to advance. The second lieutenant who brought the order took one look at Gibbons' Press insignia and said in shock: "What are you doing here?"

Gibbons replied: "Looking for a big story."

"If I were you I'd be 40 miles south of this place," the lieutenant told him.

"And then we went over," Gibbons wrote, "There are really no heroics about it. There is no bugle call, no sword waiving, no dramatic enunciation of catchy commands, no theatracalism—it's just plain get up and go over. And it is done just the same as one would walk across a peaceful wheat field out in Iowa."

The Marines, with Gibbons observing from behind, reached the woods after a quick charge that afternoon and their rifles, grenades, handguns, and bayonets lay waste to an enemy hiding in the wood. The men, organized in platoons, advanced in open order, ten to 12 feet between them. Squads would advance 50 feet and drop, flattening to the earth for dear life, then another squad would rise and make another run at the enemy. The first and third wave would be automatic rifle squads while the second and fourth were rifle grenadier squads.

Under the direction of Major John Berry, the Marines were ordered to the next goal, a triangle-shaped field 200 yards wide and 100 yards deep. As they moved from newly captured woods, they saw a number of long dead French soldiers and many newly killed and wounded Marines.

Gibbons recalled the field as "perfectly flat and covered in a young crop of oats between ten and fifteen inches high."

On the far side were entrenched German machine gunners, aiming their lethal Machinegewehr 08s. Gibbons couldn't see the crews but noticed that leaves on branches above the enemy gunners "vibrated with the fire as the tops of the young oats waved and swayed with the streams of lead that swept across."

Major Berry ordered a charge, telling his men to advance at ten to 15 yard intervals. Berry led the way with Gibbons right behind.

"Then the woods about us began to rattle fiercely," Gibbons wrote. "We began to see the dust puffs that bullets kicked up in the dirt around our feet."

They were well beyond the center of the field when the German frontal fire was joined by an unexpected machine gun from the left, a not uncommon German tactic. Marines dove to the ground. Major Berry screamed: "My hand's gone!" Gibbons yelled for the major to get down and began to creep towards the wounded officer. "I was not mistaken about the intensity of fire that swept the field. It was terrific," Gibbons wrote.

"And then it happened. The lighted end of a cigarette touched me in the fleshy part of my upper left arm. That was all. It just felt like a sudden burn and nothing more. The bullet had gone into the bicep of the upper arm and exited.

"Then the second one hit. It nicked the top of my left shoulder. And again came the burning sensation. Only this time the area affected seemed larger." To his shock, his arm still seemed to work.

Gibbons continued to crawl forward to Berry, concerned the officer was dying. He yelled encouragements as he inched. "And then the third one struck me. In order to keep as close to the ground as possible I had swung my chin to the right so that I was pushing forward with my left cheek against the ground...."

"Then there came a crash. It sounded to me like someone had dropped a glass bottle into a porcelain bathtub. A barrel of whitewash tipped over and it seemed that everything in the world turned white."

Ever the reporter, Gibbons made mental notes. "I did not know yet where I had been hit or what the bullet had done. I knew that I was still knowing things. I did not know whether I was alive or dead but I did know that my mind was still working. I was still mentally taking notes on every second."

"Am I dead?" he wondered.

"I didn't laugh or even smile when I asked myself the question without putting it in words. I wanted to know.... The shock had lifted my head off the ground but I had immediately replaced it as close to the soil as possible. My twice punctured left arm was laying alongside my body." He tried to move his left hand. His fingers wiggled. Same for his left foot. "Then I knew I was alive."

With his good hand he checked his head wound. His hand came away bloody. The left side of his face hurt terribly. He couldn't see from the side and his left eyelid wouldn't work.

The Germans had pinned down the Marines at mid-field. Ten yards from Gibbons an unconscious man moaned and flailed until a Machinegewehr 08 burst ended his troubles forever. Some of those 7.92 mm slugs came close to the reporter. Despite the withering fire, the wounded Berry successfully dashed to a patch of woods and its blessed cover.

Hartzell, hugging the ground near Gibbons, asked if Gibbons was hit. Gibbons said he was shot in the head, but didn't think it was too bad. Hartzell said he was coming over to look at the wound. "You damn fool, if you do anything don't move in my direction," Gibbons barked. "I think they think I am dead."

Gibbons' helmet, damaged when a German machine gun bullet hit a flat surface on the ground and ricocheted through it after tearing through his left eye and eyelid. He thereafter wore a knitted white eye patch, made by his mother, which became his trademark. The helmet is part of the Fogler Collection at the University of Maine.

The pair, each expecting to die, vowed to contact one another's spouse if he should survive. They repeated each other's addresses several times trying to commit them to memory.

The sun would not set for three hours. They decided to wait for darkness to try to crawl to safety. "Those three hours were long in passing," wrote Gibbons. "With the successive volleys that swept the field, I sometimes lost hope that I would ever survive it. It seemed to me that if three German bullets had found me within the space of fifteen minutes, I could hardly expect to spend three hours without receiving the fatal one."

Gibbons could try to hug the ground even closer but he couldn't stop the moaning and cries of the wounded and dying leathernecks. One he likened to a stranded calf moaning for its mother.

Finally, darkness descended with its lifeline of hope. Hartzell crawled over to Gibbons and examined his skull. Gibbons saw his comrade's grimace. Gibbons' eyeball was hanging by its nerves.

"I did not know then, as I know now, that a bullet striking the ground immediately under my left cheek bone, had ricocheted upward, going completely through the left eye and then crashing out through my forehead, leaving the eyeball and the upper eyelid completely halved, the lower eyelid torn away, and a compound fracture of the skull."

Gibbons had lost much blood and was terribly weak. Hartzell helped him along as they escaped that day of hell. It took them 20 minutes to crawl to their own lines.

But Gibbons finally had the answer to his boyhood question.

"That's how it feels to be shot," he wrote.

CHAPTER 9
Back Behind Friendly Lines

Once Gibbons and Hartzell reached the relative safety of the Allied line in the woods from which they came, Gibbons began to feel his head throbbing horribly. He had thought he was dying; now he had to focus on staying alive and getting care. All Hartzell had to bandage his companion's fractured, bleeding skull and hanging eyeball, was Gibbons' dirty silk handkerchief.

Hartzell helped steer the staggering correspondent about a mile behind the woods. There they found a small relief dugout where they found a medic.

The soldier peeled away the reddening handkerchief but there was no water to clean the wound. The medic explained he had given it away to thirsty soldiers. The duo stumbled rearward another half mile where they came upon the edge of another wooded area where dying and wounded soldiers lay in stretchers. Army doctors circulated while German rounds thundered in the trees, overriding the cries and moans. "Hartzell stretched me out on the ground and soon had a doctor bending over me," wrote Gibbons. "The doctor removed the eye bandage, took one look at what was beneath it and then replaced it. I remember this distinctly because at the time I made a mental note that the doctor apparently considered my head wound beyond anything he could repair…. He located the three [other] bullet holes, two in the arm and one across the top of the shoulder, and bound them up with bandages."

The correspondent and Hartzell continued their excruciating journey as Gibbons staggered and stumbled. Fortuitously, an ambulance heading to the rear appeared behind them. Its driver told Hartzell four wounded soldiers filled the ambulance, three men with legs shattered by bullets, another approaching death because of a lung wound. Hartzell talked the driver into allowing Gibbons to sit up front while Hartzell

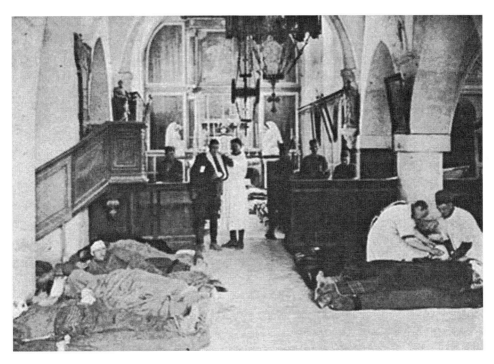

Catholic church where Gibbons was initially treated for his head wound and two arm wounds.

The church today.

stood on the running board. The road was cratered nearly to impassability, and there were ten miles to travel to find a doctor. The driver polled his passengers about speeding over the excruciatingly damaged path to save the one soldier's life. "There was not a minute's silence. The three broken leg cases responded almost in unison," wrote Gibbons. "Go as fast as you can. And we did."

Gibbons arrived at a makeshift hospital in a Catholic church at Lucy-le-Bocage. Injured and dying Marines and doughboys lay on stretchers where pews once stood for pious villagers with Rosaries. The Allies and their foes had traded control of this building four times. By now Hartzell was carrying Gibbons, who was groggy from blood loss. "My God, look what they are bringing in," a man said upon seeing him.

Gibbons' wounds were more than the ramshackle facility could manage. An ammunition truck carrying 20 wounded was leaving for a more sophisticated facility. There, a doctor examined the reporter, concluding he was a lost cause, and assigned him to the charnel ward. Hartzell was having none of that. He wrestled Gibbons onto yet another ambulance and had him taken to the U.S. Military Base Hospital at Neuilly-sur-Seine near Paris, where doctors were not as peremptory. They said they would work on him but for a time left him alone—with his fears.

"Was the operation to be a serious one or a minor one?" he wondered. "Would they have to operate on my skull? How about my arm? Would there be an amputation? How about the other eye? Would I ever see again?" No one had explained how bad his wounds were. Their reflexive conviviality—'You'll be all right, old man!'—had rung hollow. "It had seemed too professionally optimistic to satisfy me and my doubts still remained."

Then he met Major Charles Powers. The surgeon put a firm hand on Gibbons' shoulder and reassured him about the procedure he was about to perform: repairing a compound skull fracture and removing his left eye. "I like your voice," Gibbons said. "It sounds like my father's." Surely trying to distract himself by reverting to newsgathering mode, Gibbons reported his reactions to the impending surgery. Anesthesia might knock him cold, but he was determined to track his interior journey.

"My mental note taking continued as the anesthetist worked over me with ether," he wrote. "As I began breathing the fumes I remember that my senses were keenly making observations on every sensation I experienced. The thought even went through my mind that it would be rather an unusual thing to report completely the impression of coma. The suggestion became a determination and I became keyed up to everything going on about me."

The ether triggered a familiar hallucination, one he had when given gas by his Chicago dentist—a visit from a misshapen creature with twinkling eyes. "I laughed outright, laughed hilariously. I recognized the man. The last time I had seen him was when he stepped out of a gas tank on the 18th floor of an office building in Chicago...." A few more flickerings and Gibbons lost consciousness, waking with a repaired skull but an eyelid so damaged it could never hold a prosthetic eyeball.

During the hospitalization in Paris, Gibbons wrote home, offering an upbeat view, probably to calm his mother and to avoid the army censors' scissors.

"I am perfectly easy and without pain and I have everything in the world that I would want or ask for," Gibbons wrote. "I have had a most remarkable experience, which has cost me not a single regret.... My wounds are healing fine; the doctors report them in the best of condition. My right eye is absolutely unaffected, although not permitted to use it as yet...."

"In this ward there are many brave fellows. Some have lost legs, some have lost arms and some are paralyzed and some are pitted with particles of shrapnel. It is seldom they give into their pain, and never do they complain of their lot. Their only regret is that most of them never will have another opportunity to return to the front. They are fine company, mother—Irishmen, Jews, Poles, Italians. But, my God, what men! They are the new Americans, born in the hell of battle. Don't worry about me, mother. I am sound in mind and body and very fortunate to be."

The *Tribune* printed Gibbons' letter as part of its coverage, which also quoted from a telegram Gibbons received from his father: "Thanks

Front-page drawing in the Chicago Tribune of Gibbons going into battle with the Marines.

British Prime Minister Lloyd George, who expressed sympathy to Gibbons about his eye when the two met after Gibbons returned to work on the German front. Said Gibbons: "It only takes one eye, Mr. George, to see the Kaiser's finish...."

for your good right eye. Thousands of Gibbonses and millions of other Americans are with you. Up and at them. Your mother is with me. Mother says you are her hero. Speedy Recovery. Love from All. Dad." Gibbons recovered with remarkable speed–within six weeks he was back at the front covering the recapture of Chateau-Thierry by U.S. and French troops. On that front, Gibbons met British Prime Minister Lloyd George. Reporter Paul West, who had written for the *New York Herald*, described their conversation: "I'm sorry to see that you have lost an eye," said George. "Don't mind a bit," Gibbons said. "It only takes one eye, Mr. George, to see the Kaiser's finish after this great day."

Prior to his wounds, he wondered privately to his brother whether his public bravado was doing enough for his country. He said he sometimes wished to fight the Germans as a pilot. But he said his journalism mattered, too. "At times I have the discouraged feeling that I am no more than a brazen trumpeter, standing in safety and letting out metallic brays to urge the other fellows on but then again I feel that if there is anything I can do by my writings that will awake America sooner and thereby end the war quicker, even though it be only as much as one day, I will have done a national service far greater than any that might be bought with the sacrifice of my life."

Gibbons had Isabella at his side during the recovery. She had shipped over in May of 1917, serving as his private secretary and volunteering. She joined him in the hospital right after his wounding. How much comfort she gave, though, is unclear. New York *World Tribune* columnist Heywood Broun recalled Isabella, known as Izzy, as a "large and beautiful Swede" with whom Gibbons "quarreled quite a lot during the war, and I do remember that Izzy was very jealous." He recalled the time American actress and songstress Elsie Janis visited the hospital where Gibbons was recuperating. "Just as she started to sing a song at the foot of Floyd's cot Izzy wandered in and said, 'Who is this woman?' There was a rumpus."

Gibbons during his recovery.

Gibbons and an Army photographer while recovering from wounds.

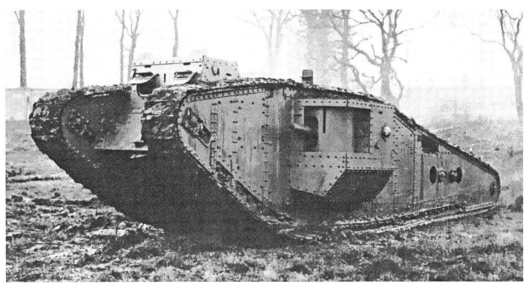

British World War I tank. Gibbons rode one into battle. He described the tank as "a cross between an armadillo and a steel jail," which made "an inferno of sound." The British were first to develop the tank, designed to attack Germans in trenches. When battle action was slow, Gibbons wasn't above instigating it. "Isn't there some way you can stir them up a little," he asked a French officer near Reims, who complied by ordering his men to fire grenade rifles.

Gibbons and wife Isabella Pehrman in 1917. She had joined him in Paris in May of 1917 before his wounding and worked as his secretary and later with the Red Cross. Gibbons was unemployed and broke when he impetuously married her in 1914 in Chicago, an act he quickly regretted. Their relationship further frayed during his convalescence, when she openly became jealous of female visitors. After considerable private hostility from Gibbons, the two divorced after the war, with Gibbons declaring for public consumption that Mrs. Gibbons was "the finest woman I know."

CHAPTER 10
The Marines

The troops of the United States Marine Corps were not always *The Marines*. Yes, they had fought in the halls of Montezuma during the Mexican-American war in 1846 and their antecedents battled pirates on the shores of Tripoli in 1804. But few outside the Marines' own ranks and the U.S. Navy officers aboard the ships with Marine complements thought much of the men who served as the Navy's on-board army and little else. Descended from a British unit with the same name assigned as sharpshooters aboard Royal Navy vessels, America's Marines since their 1775 creation had always been on the fringes of the national military establishment. Corps leadership had to regularly counter attempts at disbanding the doughty little force.

In 1908, President Theodore Roosevelt, seeing the Corps as superfluous, sought reform. His executive order of that year sharply limited the leathernecks (in the 19th century they wore high leather collars) largely to protective duty, and the Administration seemed bound to consign them to oblivion. But interservice rivalry saved the day. The Navy, incensed at the idea of U.S. Army soldiers guarding its bases, successfully pushed to keep the Marines. Congress overrode Roosevelt's order and the Corps survived to fight a great many other days.

American entry into the Great War sharpened the Corps' focus and gave it a raison d'etre. However, American Expeditionary Force Commander General John J. Pershing was disinclined to let the Marines ship overseas at all. Marine Corps Commandant George Barnett prevailed upon Secretary of the Navy Josephus Daniels and Chief of Naval Operations William Benson to let the Corps join the Army overseas. They approached the War Department and won the assignment, without Pershing ever being consulted.

Pershing got revenge for being outmaneuvered. Instead of letting them into the fray, Pershing made the leathernecks military police and longshoremen, unloading transports and directing Army traffic headed to the front. He also put an Army man in charge of them. With only 9,000 Marines in Europe, Black Jack could disperse them easily enough among the two million other Americans of the AEF.

The Marines performed as ordered but their officers bristled, making it clear they wanted at the Hun. They hoped and prayed and finagled for the opportunity to show the Corps' military mettle.

That break came in early June 1918 at Belleau Wood, a former hunting preserve, where the Germans were making an all-out effort to defeat the Allies before the Americans could get their troops to that site. A German offensive begun in March was making considerable headway until Belleau Wood. Fighting for the U.S. were the U.S. 3rd and 2nd Army Divisions, which included a Brigade of Marines. They joined with Allied forces against German units from the 237th, 10th, 197th, 87th and 28th Divisions.

The placeholder story Gibbons filed before being wounded so badly ran in the *Tribune* as he had drafted it, describing a great American success with particular praise for the fighting leathernecks, whom he referred to as "the Marines." "In this fighting and struggle of the last three days," Gibbons wrote in this placeholder story before being shot, "much credit redounds to the United States Marines, who have been steadily in the first line."

He continued to heap praise on the leathernecks after his wounding at Belleau Wood. Interviewed by his own newspaper as he lay recovering in the hospital, Gibbons said: "Those Marines are wonderful, perfectly wonderful. Nothing could stop them. They went over the top four times in the afternoon under a perfect storm of machine gun fire and drove the Germans before them. They set their bayonets and went to it like they had been used to it all their lives and cleaned out nest after nest of machine guns with which the woods seemed alive."

When German bullets felled Gibbons, early reports had him dead, according to one historian. It so moved the Army censor handling Gibbons' placeholder article that he allowed the story to pass unaltered, even though censorship rules required he eliminate the Marine reference. Another historian said Army censors let the mention stand because the Corps was a separate branch of service. Whatever the reason, censors let Gibbons' story through. Thanks to his name and the *Tribune*'s distribution chain, hundreds of papers across the country carried the story that seemed to say Marine defiance kept the Kaiser from marching beneath the Arc de Triomphe. "U.S. MARINES SMASH HUNS," a *Tribune* headline read June 6. "MARINES WIN HOT BATTLE," read another June 7. *The New York Times* reported: "OUR MARINES, GAIN MILE AT VEIULLY, RESUME DRIVE AT NIGHT, FOE LOSING HEAVILY."

All this ink for mere Marines infuriated the Army brass. "The press reports of the 2nd (Army) Division's fight shouted Marines, Marines, Marines until the word resounded over the whole earth, and made the inhabitants thereof, except for a few Americans in the Army in France, believe there was nothing …indeed in front of the Germans but Marines," Army Maj. General Robert L. Bullard later wrote. "General Pershing came to visit me at dinner and I said, 'I see the 2nd Marines (emphasizing 2nd as if the division was all Marines) have won the war at Belleau Wood.' 'Yes,' he answered dryly." And when France's Prime Minister, Georges Clemenceau, visited the 2nd Division headquarters after the battle, Army commanders made certain no leathernecks were present, a snub Marine historians still invoke. The Army did, however, order that henceforth Belleau Wood be referred to as Bois de la Brigade de Marine.

Inspecting the battle site also was Navy Secretary Franklin Roosevelt, according to *The United States Marines Corps* by John Selby and Michael Roffe.

He was so impressed he allowed enlisted men for the first time to wear the Marine emblem on their collar like their officers and praised the Corps in a letter to Secretary of Defense Josephus Daniels. "American and French commanders are equally enthusiastic over the magnificent showing. Have also visited Belleau Wood, a most difficult position which the Marines held against German troops and finally cleared," he wrote.

German intelligence also took note of the Marines in a report. "The 2nd American Division must be considered a very good one and may be perhaps reckoned storm troops. The different attacks on Belleau Wood were carried out with bravery and dash. The moral effect of our gunfire cannot seriously impede the advance of the American riflemen."

Floyd Gibbons further mythologized the Marines by lionizing Sergeant Major Daniel Joseph Daly at Belleau Wood. Daly was the quintessential Leatherneck, a man who came to WW I with not one but two Congressional Medals of Honor on his chest, one for courage in the Boxer Rebellion in 1900 in China, and one for fighting insurgents in Haiti in 1915. In France, Gibbons observed the diminutive Daly poised to lead a charge in the face of blistering gun fire.

In his account, Gibbons recalled that prior to encountering Daly, his ideal for combative spirit was a French sergeant in Victor Hugo's *Les Miserables* battling the English. Asked to surrender, that sergeant used a vile one-word epithet as his reply before he was killed.

Gibbons found a new ideal at Belleau Wood. "…An old gunnery sergeant commanded the platoon in the absence of the lieutenant, who had been shot and was out of the fight. This old sergeant was a Marine veteran. His cheeks were bronzed with the wind and sun of the seven seas. The service bar across his left breast showed that he had fought in the Philippines, in Santo Domingo, at the walls of Pekin, and in the streets of Vera Cruz. I make no apologies for his language. Even if Hugo were not my precedent, I would make no apologies. To me his words were classic, if not sacred."

"As the minute for the advance arrived, he arose from the trees first and jumped out onto the exposed edge of that field that ran with lead, across which he and his men were to charge. Then he turned to give the charge order to the men of his platoon—his mates—the men he loved. He said:

"COME ON, YOU SONS-O'-BITCHES! DO YOU WANT TO LIVE FOREVER?"

Marine Sergeant Major Daniel Joseph Daly, made a Marine icon by Gibbons, who quoted him when leading a charge at Belleau Wood: "COME ON, YOU SONS-O'-BITCHES! DO YOU WANT TO LIVE FOREVER?" Daly's battle phrase is etched into the Marine Corps Museum's Rotunda in Quantico, Va.

Gibbons' account of Sergeant Daly's declaration is beloved among Marines, ranked by at least one historian as with the battle phrases "Remember the Alamo" and "I have not yet begun to fight." Daly survived World War I and became a bank guard, certainly a quite intimidating one. He died in 1937; his name and famous declaration are etched into the Marine Museum's Rotunda in Quantico, Va. Gibbons was responsible for transmitting them to posterity.

Gibbons, too, is credited with being the first to report that after Belleau Wood German soldiers so feared the Marines that they called them *Teufel Hunden*, or "devil dogs." The Marines still cherish that sobriquet and their mascot to this day is a bulldog. Marines and others still debate the term's origins. Writer H. L. Mencken claimed Gibbons made up the tale out of whole cloth.

The Marines were happy to have Gibbons as their chronicler. When Gibbons, towards the end of the war, returned stateside to lecture against ending the war prematurely, a press release put out by the tour's agent cast the Marines as the conflict's heroes. Gibbons, the release said, had returned to tell "the people of this country how the 'Devil Dogs' from America saved Paris" and noted the reporter would be appearing in some places under Marine auspices.

The press agent goes to lengths in stating Gibbons' bona fides for his lectures. He cites his Mexican and *Laconia* experiences and says Gibbons reported with the British in Flanders and the French in the Argonne and Champagne districts. The release credits him with being the first correspondent to cross the old Alsatian frontier and for being with the Americans when they crossed into German territory. As if Gibbons' eye patch wouldn't be reminder enough of his valor, the agent points out that Gibbons flew in a British bombing plane and took anti-aircraft fire while in an American plane. He also once rode against Germans in a claustrophobic British tank that Gibbons described as "a cross between an armadillo and a steel jail."

Gibbons' praise for the leathernecks at Belleau Wood is certainly well founded, if only for the tremendous losses they took. A total of 1,087 Marines died there, including 33 officers. In his book, *Miracle at Belleau*

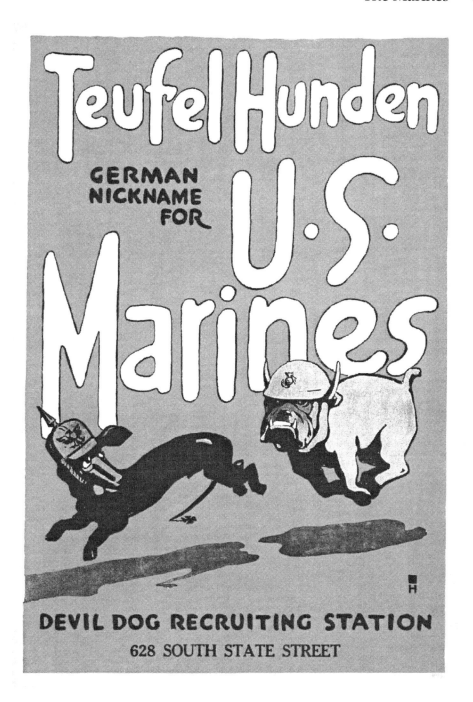

The Marine Corps' role in the victory over Germany at Belleau Wood was emphasized by Gibbons and then trumpeted by his newspaper and others after he was shot. Previously the Marines were seen as largely an adjunct to the Navy, and their existence had been threated numerous times in the budget process. Gibbons was credited with first reporting that Germans called the Marines "Devil Dogs," a term they cherish to this day. The bulldog has become their mascot.

Wood, author Alan Axelrod describes a lieutenant colonel, asked afterwards how the Marines had fared, replying sadly, "There aren't any more Marines."

"And so it must have seemed," said Axelrod, "to one who had lived through the thick of the fight and saw the fall of so many he commanded there. Yet in the hell of the Belleau Wood, the Corps had not died. The reputation of the Marines, America's fiercest warriors, the nation's elite fighting force, was forged in the battle. After Belleau Wood, the Marines claimed the right to be regarded as the American vanguard, the first to fight, and if necessary the last to leave. The Marine Corps emerged from Belleau Wood in possession of a legend unlike any the Army or Navy could claim. The legend would animate the Corps through the next world war and through the wars in Korea, Vietnam and Iraq."

In time, that legend enveloped Gibbons himself. In 1941 he was named the Corps' first honorary Marine by the Marine Corps League. Veterans of Foreign Wars Post 500 in New York City was named after him, as was a Liberty war transport ship in 1944. Though the honorary Marine award was posthumous, Gibbons might have prized it above all others, Shelley Mitchell-Schaff, Gibbons' grand-niece, said in an interview.

The Corps again celebrated Gibbons in 2009, when the Marine Museum opened in Quantico. The facility's Belleau Wood exhibit places considerable focus on the role of Floyd Gibbons, including an exhibit showing Gibbons batting out a news story in a foxhole as the battle swells around him. A recorded voice reads the copy, interlaced with the clatter of war and the clacking of a typewriter. Gibbons is also included in exhibits at the Smithsonian and the Newseum in Washington, D.C.

Correspondent Floyd Gibbons in a display in the Marine Corps Museum in Quantico, Va. (Photo courtesy of the Museum)

The author, left, and World War I guide Gilles Lagin, an honorary Marine, examine the scene near where Gibbons was shot.

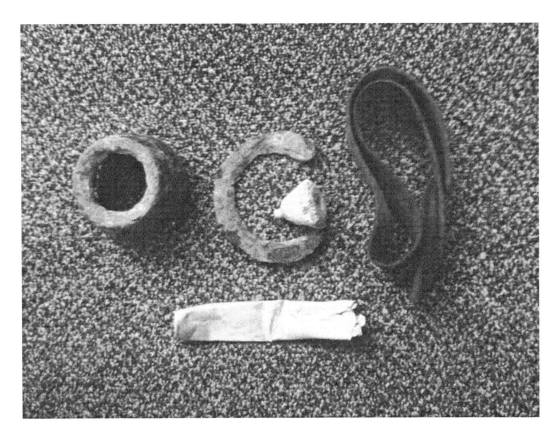

Bomb fragments, a mule shoe, a Marine toothbrush holder and a French soldier's belt found by Lagin when walking near the site of Gibbons' wounding.

CHAPTER 11
Lecturing for the Cause

Wounded in combat and a powerful witness on behalf of the Allies, Gibbons in August 1918 was recruited by Allied Commander Marshal Foch and AEF Leader Blackjack Pershing to stump in the U.S. against ending the war. A German-proposed overture would only give back Belgium, Alsace-Lorraine and have the Kaiser pay indemnities. Foch and Pershing thought this insufficient and distrusted the Germans who they knew they had on the ropes. They wanted Gibbons on the speaking circuit to dilute American politicians' pandering to a populace clamoring to get their boys home. Gibbons was also tasked with encouraging audiences to buy Liberty Bonds supporting the war effort.

Gibbons and the *Tribune* happily urged on the war, supported by 17 other American combat correspondents who unanimously voted Gibbons their point man in the states. The vote was equal parts affectionate concern—Gibbons clearly needed time away from the front to recover from his injuries—and blatant self-interest—with their main competitor on the hustings at home, his rivals stood to score more scoops of their own. To make clear whose water he would be carrying, Gibbons, before returning stateside, wrote an article about Pershing that he submitted to the general for his approval. "I am sincerely trusting that it meets with your favor and that you will permit its use against the workings of the anti-war forces in America," the reporter said in an accompanying note, adding that he had triple-spaced the draft so Pershing could make any changes "that might recommend themselves to you." This would be considered unethical today.

Gibbons boarded an army transport ship in France on Aug. 15; en route he rested for his lecture tour. He landed in New York seven days later to greetings from a Marine Corps honor guard and a scrum of reporters and photographers.

At an impromptu press conference the first question, about a medal the French had awarded him, caught Gibbons off guard. "What is this Croix de Guerre stuff..." asked Gibbons. The French had announced during Gibbons' voyage that he was to receive the Croix de Guerre with Palm. France issued no higher battle award to foreigners. In time the list of Americans joining Gibbons would include future General George Patton and U. S. Medal of Honor winner Captain Eddie Rickenbacker, the aerial ace. Also getting the medal was log-cabin-born Army Sergeant Alvin York, the war's most famous hero for leading an attack which yielded 32 enemy machine guns, 20 dead Germans and 132 prisoners. Gibbons and York jointly spoke on tour at times.

In its coverage, the *Tribune* quoted its famous reporter as downplaying the medal and his wounds. "We cannot write about what our men are doing unless we do it ourselves and we cannot tell how they feel unless we feel it too, so let's cut out what happened to me," he said. "I have come home...to tell the American people what is going on in Europe and why we should keep on with the war." Former President Theodore Roosevelt invited Gibbons to his Long Island home to tell what he knew of the death of Roosevelt's son, Quentin, 20, an AEF pilot shot down in his Nieuport 28 on July 14 and buried in France. After a sorrowful visit with the old man, Gibbons began his tour in his hometown, Washington, D.C. Before addressing a crowd at the National Theater, the correspondent met with President Wilson to discuss the war, telling the commander-in-chief about an episode at the American hospital near Paris while he was recovering from his wounds. Gibbons asked one of his ward mates his thoughts about the president. "That guy has hair on his chest," the soldier said.

That night at the theatre, the Marines again were front and center with their man Floyd. Commandant Major General George Barnett was to introduce Gibbons before an audience surely dotted with relatives and friendly faces from his days as a paperboy, Gonzaga cadet and Georgetown student. Gibbons spoke to the National Press Club prior to that event, and the *Washington Post* coverage of the speeches appears to stick to the press release, emphasizing his local connections and Gibbons' credibility. "In addition to giving his audiences graphic pictures of what

France's Croix de Guerre, the highest battle award given to foreigners. Gibbons received word of his from the press after his ship docked in New York in August 1918. He was beginning a nationwide tour at the request of the Allies to oppose ending the war too quickly.

modern warfare is like on the west front," the *Post* reporter wrote, "he will also expose many of the schemes of the Germans."

From Washington, Gibbons took a train to New York to speak at Carnegie Hall. Alderman President Alfred E. Smith, future governor and presidential candidate, introduced his fellow Irish-American in one of two talks Gibbons made from the famous stage Sept. 8. *The New York Times* described his remarks as "vivid." "Let us finish the fight, for we can finish it," said Gibbons, "Hold fast at home."

Gibbons next appeared in another of his hometowns, Chicago, again with a Marine contingent, but also to receive his Croix de Guerre with Palm in a scene his paper lovingly and proudly chronicled.

> "Floyd Gibbons, battle-scarred war correspondent for the *Tribune*, met yesterday morning at the Illinois Central depot by a Great Lakes band, a company of colonels, a major and a captain or two, a squad of marines, the Lieutenant Governor of Illinois, judges, politicians and an applauding multitude, stepped from the train, grinned boyishly, then threw his one good arm around an elderly woman, bent down, and—

> "'Mother!' he said, as he kissed her. Then he shook, with that one good arm, the hand of his father, E.T. Gibbons, Sr., and embraced a sister, Mrs. Margaret Gibbons Chapman, and the naval band joyously struck up 'Home, Sweet Home.'

> "M. Antonio Barthelemy, French Consul to Chicago, who a few minutes later was to present him with the Croix de Guerre with Palm given by the French government, took step beside him. The procession swung out into Michigan Boulevard.

> "'I am thinking that it's rather funny,' said Floyd Gibbons with a laugh. 'Here I am with all of those police ahead of me. In the old days they used to always be behind, chasing.'"

One of the saddest parts of his trip home came when he was invited by former President Theodore Roosevelt to his Long Island residence to tell him details of the death of Roosevelt's pilot son, Quentin, 20, who had been shot down and buried in France. Gibbons had previously interviewed Roosevelt in 1912 in Milwaukee where Roosevelt recovered from an unsuccessful assassination attempt while running for president on the Progressive Party ticket.

Wreckage and body of Quentin Roosevelt, whose Nieuport 28 had been shot down July 14, 1918. The Germans made great propaganda use of his death. Like Gibbons, Roosevelt was awarded a Croix de Guerre with Palm.

Backtracking through his career, Gibbons followed his Chicago homecoming with one in Minneapolis, which out-roared the Windy City in its affection, according to another of the reporter's alma maters, the *Minneapolis Tribune:*

"Today was 'home-town' day for Floyd Gibbons. He was kept busy from early morning, shortly after he doffed his pajamas at the Radisson and put on his khaki uniform, greeting old friends... 'Say, this isn't real! I'm somewhere over there in France helping push up the daisies, and this is all a dream!'

"Floyd Gibbons was speaking. He had just stepped off the train at the Milwaukee station about noon yesterday, to be greeted by syncopated blasts from the Minneapolis police band....

"'Sure does my heart good to see all these places again,' remarked Gibbons, gazing down Washington Avenue. His eyes roved toward the place 'under the clock' at City Hall where prisoners were lodged. A white-haired woman in the window, tears streaming down her face, was throwing kisses in the general direction of the khaki-clad war veteran.

"'Matron Schaeffer,' he exclaimed, waving back to her, and making a feeble attempt to shout 'hello.' Somehow or other, Gibbons can't yell the way he used to. His war injuries did that.

"A wave of applause greeted his entrance at Arcadia. Inside were more than 1,500 Liberty Loan workers and outside were several hundred that couldn't get in. He was finally permitted to sit down and eat. It was a patriotic luncheon.

"In fact, the first thing he said when he sat down was: 'Just like in the army!'

"There were beans and brown bread, and a hot bun with butter, coffee with a teaspoon of sugar, and slices of lemon cream pie. His eyes kept roving over the audience instead of over his plate, however, and he negotiated only the pie and coffee, with three cigarettes...."

"Then Gibbons spoke. For 25 minutes, the huge audience sat enthralled while intimate little tales of boys from the Northwest, fighting in France, were related. Outbursts of cheering and laughing and periods of absolute silence punctuated the talk.

"'Last time I was in this building,' he began, 'I had to pay a dime to get in, and the slogan was 'On with the dance' instead of 'Buy Liberty Bonds.' It was the Dreamland Dancehall then.'"

He told his audience he had brought a message from Colonel George E. Leach of the 151st Field Artillery, formerly the First Minnesota Infantry. Gibbons recalled how he met him.

"One night just before I started back," he said, "I drove along in the dark up to an old, half-fallen wall back of which was what remained of a mill.

"The thunder of the big guns and the continuous roar of the smaller arms, the flashes of flame, and the star shells weren't far off. They were close enough to make it mighty uncomfortable for a fellow to be out in the open.

"Up a rickety old staircase, half a shot away, with big holes in the wall, I went. Up in the attic of the place I stopped. It was headquarters of the 151st...."

Gibbons asked the Colonel what his message home would be. "Tell them that the 151st is the finest, cleanest, fightingest, most loyal regiment of true Americans in France!" Leach replied.

Gibbons told his audience that day in Minneapolis that prior to the war there had been whispers that Americans of Scandinavian descent weren't supportive of the war. "Let the people who said that look at the casualty lists," Leach told Gibbons.

"The war is not yet won," Gibbons said, "and the Germans are retreating from France after fighting for every foot of ground. The peace they ask for is a German peace."

"They want a peace in which they can retain their armed forces, their undefeated armies. They are willing to give up Belgium, northern France, and even Alsace and Lorraine," he said.

Gibbons that day was prescient about the heights of horror to which Germany eventually could ascend. He said if a premature peace is reached, "in 25 years Germany will again prove a menace to the world, and will make every attempt to destroy her present enemies in a war that would surpass in rottenness and horror even this one." The Allies got a peace on their terms but Hitler came to power in part by railing against what he saw as their draconian nature.

Gibbons had an unwelcome rival for public attention as he toured. The so-called Spanish influenza epidemic, which began in June 1918, continued to race across the country and the world. The flu, which oddly took its biggest toll on young adults, was spread more quickly by the increased travel during the war. Medicines for it were still some years away and the results were devastating. As much as 6% of the world's population succumbed including some 675,000 Americans. To combat it, almost all public gatherings in the U.S. were banned and Gibbons' speaking tour was cut short when he got to Omaha, Neb. Oct. 15 after speeches in Rockhurst, Ill., and Sioux City, Iowa.

Silenced by the epidemic, Gibbons holed up in Atlantic City, New Jersey, to work on his book entitled *And They Thought We Wouldn't Fight*, a firsthand account of the American role in the Great War. As always, writing against the clock and the inevitable competition from other correspondents, he finished his draft in three weeks, composing a narrative of the strategic and tactical events of 1917-18 punctuated by

In Grant Park, Chicago, for the award ceremony of the Croix de Guerre with Palm. Gibbons was accompanied by Marines, state and French officials and to his rear, his sister, Margaret.

Gibbons receives the medal from his mother, Emma, as his father, Edward, looks on between the two.

chats with the French civilians, doughboys, and Marines. Gibbons hoped to capitalize on the fame his coverage of the *Laconia* sinking and his wounds at Belleau Wood had brought. He included his coverage and thoughts on each episode in the 410-page volume published by George H. Doran Company in 1918.

The Allies and the Germans declared the Armistice on Nov. 11 as Gibbons finished his book. The Germans were faced with certain defeat and capitulated to allied demands for surrender. Gibbons' own wartime articles and those about him, coupled with his speaking tour and the coverage it engendered, helped make him the most famous war correspondent of the era. His handsome Irish face and trademark white eye patch—knitted by his mother—now made him tremendously memorable. His book as of some four years later had sold 35,000 copies, a not insubstantial number in that era but no best-seller either. The war for many Americans, at least as Gibbons reported it, was better left forgotten. The pain was too great.

Though much of Europe was in shambles, the *Chicago Tribune's* management saw an opportunity. The war-time Paris edition was in place and could easily become a peace-time daily. Gibbons was named its editor and director of the *Trib's* Foreign Service, launching the paper and its most famous reporter onto an even larger international stage.

Army Sergeant Alvin York, one of the most decorated soldiers of World War I. Gibbons and York spoke together on stage in support of the war. York had led an attack on German machine gun nests, capturing 32 machine guns, killing at least 20 men, and capturing 132 others.

President Woodrow Wilson, whom Gibbons met with in the White House before beginning a speaking tour opposing ending the war prematurely. Gibbons later produced and narrated a documentary on Wilson's presidency entitled "Woodrow Wilson's Big Decision." It played as a "short" to go with longer features at movie houses.

General John Pershing, commander of the American Expeditionary Force during World War I. Gibbons became friends with Pershing when covering him as he chased Pancho Villa in Mexico. Pershing asked Gibbons to return to the U.S. to speak against ending the war too quickly. (Photo by the author's grandmother, Octavia Yeomans, made at U.S. victory parade in Washington, D.C., Sept. 17, 1919)

Pershing, leading the parade. (Yeomans photo)

The French 75 mm that fired the first shot by Americans in the war. Gibbons documented the firing on the scene, listing the soldiers manning the gun and kept the shell of that first shot. Years later, he presented it to the soldier who fired it. (Yeomans photo)

Gibbons, far left, with Tribune co-publisher Captain Joseph Patterson and presidential advisor and peace negotiator Bernard Baruch.

Gibbons and Tribune *Publisher Robert McCormick.*

CHAPTER 12
World's Zaniest Newspaper

As the *Paris Tribune* editor, Gibbons oversaw a revolving ensemble of reporters and editors come and go and come again, drawn to postwar Paris for its rekindled arts, nightlife and opportunities for adventure. Often as not these newshawks were undependable, mischievous and given to drink—but also brilliant, creative and driven. *Paris Tribune* reporter William Shirer, later to gain renown as a World War II historian, remembered the *Paris Trib* as the "World's Zaniest Newspaper," a play on its corporate parent's claim to be "The World's Greatest Newspaper."

The *Tribune* transformed its Army edition to a peacetime Paris edition, promoting it as the scrappy underdog to bark at the heels of the well-ensconced *New York Herald's* Paris edition. That paper was begun in 1887 by Edward Bennett, Jr., the wealthy *New York Herald* owner whose primary publishing goal, rather than profit or influence, seemed to be to remain connected to the U. S. while residing in Paris. Colonel McCormick, on the other hand, an isolationist, seemed to be focusing on profit and additional domestic prestige, which garnered little of the former but a fair amount of the latter, particularly with the famous Gibbons at the helm. Competing in the same market for English readers were the *Paris Times* and the Continental edition of the *Daily Mail* of London.

In addition to heading the *Trib* edition, Gibbons was chief correspondent and head of the parent company's foreign news service—roles he savored. Leaving administration to others or no one, he would cover events across European capitals, installing bureau chiefs in what was becoming one of the larger international newspaper foreign services. Gibbons and the *Trib* must have had some credibility because long before it was scheduled to be released, a disgruntled negotiator of the Treaty of Versailles in May of 1919 gave the paper a copy of it for publication. Scared to telegraph it home, the *Tribune* had an employee carry it back to Chicago, where a national stir ensued over a variety of controversial points.

Gibbons prided himself on concern for the American soldiers, and he used his paper to help them out. Some two million soldiers were awaiting transportation home months after the war ended and there were too few transports to take them. He began an old fashioned newspaper crusade to put pressure on the powers that be. "GET THE DOUGHBOYS HOME TOOT SWEET" read a headline. "A.E.F. + P.D.Q. = U.S.A." read another.

Trib Paris edition reporters took perverse pride in their paper's reputation for low pay, skimpy budgets, and general cantankerousness. Waverly Root described himself and his fellow staffers as "a club and a cult" where "we liked each other" and "loved putting out the paper." In a Proustian account in *Remembrance of Things Paris*, reporter Corbally Kuhn recalled that the Chicago paper's Paris edition emanated from "a single dingy room on the upper floor on the rue Lamartine—an unremarkable street…. There were no desks, merely scarred, battered plank tables to support the decrepit typewriters, of which there were never enough to go around. Rickety chairs, a telex machine, a few telephones, and a half dozen or so naked light bulbs dangling from a painted tin ceiling completed the décor."

Offsetting these conditions was the fact that "the *Trib*'s editorial room backed into the same courtyard as a cheerful, rowdy bistro. Arrangements had long since been made for buckets of cool, foaming beer to be conveyed by means of a rope from the courtyard to the editorial room to speed the flow of copy on a hot summer's night," Kuhn rhapsodized.

The paper had the "unique and irreplaceable advantage" of Floyd Gibbons' reportorial talents. By then, Kuhn said, Gibbons was "legendary, the quintessential foreign correspondent, a handsome man with a huge sense of adventure, unlimited daring and great personal courage." His work often ran on page one of what usually was a six-page broadsheet claiming a circulation of 5,000.

Budding and aspiring poets and writers worked the rim on the paper's copy desk or as proofreaders. People like Henry Miller, later to write the notorious 1934 novel *Tropic of Cancer*, and James Thurber, who was to gain fame as a humorist and cartoonist at the *New Yorker*, were on staff. Gertrude Stein and Ezra Pound freelanced contributions. Ernest Hemingway and James Joyce first gained notice in its literature reviews. F. Scott Fitzgerald, usually on a toot, sometimes would just drop in. Fitzgerald once commandeered the chief copy editor's chair and yelled, "Come on boys, let's get out the goddamned paper." Another time he and wife Zelda appeared; the novelist announced he had just been to a certain brothel and helpfully recommended its services to all assembled.

Gibbons, no stranger to a bar or a drink, once caused quite a stir in a dust-up with American ex-patriot dancer Isadora Duncan while at the Select café. Talk at the table came around to the trial of anarchists Nicola Sacco and Bartolomeo Vanzetti, who were found guilty of murder in a New England shoe factory robbery and sentenced to death. Gibbons claimed the duo was given a "fair trial," according to writer William Shirer. Duncan became furious and gave the *Trib* correspondent a "tongue lashing." Soon "sympathizers on both sides joined in and there was a fray with glasses and saucers hurled about until the police intervened to break it up," Shirer said.

Gibbons was increasingly spending time in the Paris nightspots. Izzy recalled in a letter to Gibbons the times where she went searching for him in the cafes and bars "and there were women and wine and I made scenes." Izzy herself was hospitalized for "exhaustion" several times over the next few years and, shortly after one of these episodes, Gibbons on Sept. 28, 1922, called her into his separate bedroom where he demanded an immediate and quiet divorce. She expressed shock, held out hope but some weeks later shipped out permanently for home.

His marriage notwithstanding, Gibbons in late 1922 took up with one of the most glamorous opera singers in Paris, American Mary McCormic. McCormic became known for her leading soprano roles with the Paris National Opera, not an institution known for encouraging American singers, particularly one from—appropriately enough—Yell County, Arkansas. What the Arkansas Songbird, as she was known, lacked in cosmopolitan upbringing she made up in boyfriends and marriages, Gibbons getting in on the act early. When asked by a reporter—as she faced going down the aisle for the fifth time—how often she had been married, she replied: "I marry 'em; why can't you newspapermen count 'em?"

She and Gibbons met when she brought him a formal letter of introduction from a friend of Gibbons in Paris. Oddly, she presented it in the non-businesslike basement cabaret of Harry's New York Bar. She told him she aspired to continue her Chicago Opera success in the City of Lights. The two hit it off, clearly not an uncommon occurrence for Ms. McCormic. But she insisted in an interview that she "was meeting for the first time the man who was to become the central figure of the most romantic period of my whole life." Gibbons' brother said she was the one love of Gibbons' life.

While in Paris, Gibbons also had a friendship—and a brief fling— with Dorothy Thompson, known as the First Lady of American Journalism, who bested Gibbons in several scoops for a variety of papers, not the least of which was an interview with Hitler in 1931. Gibbons himself had railed against Hitler in 1930, perhaps precluding his own shot at an interview.

While there was serious journalism being done at the Paris edition, boredom and its corollary, drink, affected the paper, with sheer fiction sometimes comically threaded among the actual news.

"Lieutenant General and Mrs. Pendelton Gray Winslow have arrived at their villa, Heart's Desire, on Cap d'Antibes, bringing with them their prize Burmese monkey, Thibault," read one such made-up squib.

Thurber had a gift for producing such pearls.

"'A man who does not pray is not a praying man,' President Coolidge today told the annual convention of Protestant Churches of America," Thurber wrote, foreshadowing the flat-affect drolleries that would make the *Onion* a worldwide sensation nearly a century later.

Playing on expatriate Americans' familiarity with a touring troupe of hirsute baseball players who bore themselves with mock-biblical seriousness, the *Trib* wrote, "Okokomino, Ind. Friday, Mr. Lysander C. Chew, head of the local House of David, was today severely injured when his beard caught in the automatic wringer of a steam laundry, where he was working incognito."

Perhaps the most outrageous such item came from the brow of Spencer Bull, a tippling deskman assigned to write up the dedication of an orphanage in Paris by the British heir apparent, Prince Edward.

"Stopping before one manly youth the prince inquired: 'What is your name, my lad?'" Bull wrote. "'None of your goddamned business, sir,' the youngster replied. At that, the Prince snatched a riding crop from his equerry and beat the boy's brains out."

Not a soul in the paper's editing, composing or proofreading chain intervened, even when some imp added the headline, "PRINCE OF WALES BEATS BOY'S BRAINS OUT WITH BLUDGEON." Gibbons took the call from London on that one, apologized to the Prince and fired Bull, who Root said thereafter "lived happily on free booze and meals offered him by admirers who wanted to meet the man who accused the Prince of Wales of murder."

Given the amount of nonsense that showed up in his paper, Gibbons clearly had a high tolerance for horseplay and shenanigans. Chicago generally did not: Gibbons "was too much concerned with his own writings and neglected the organization," his boss, Publisher Robert McCormick, complained in his memoir.

Paris Tribune *newsroom. After publishing the Army edition of the* Tribune *during World War I, its publishers continued the* Paris Tribune *as a peacetime newspaper. Gibbons was its head and chief foreign correspondent.*

Paris café society and nightlife were integral to Americans who flocked to Paris after the war. Artists and writers blossomed in the city, and the Paris Tribune *first made known or better known the works of such writers as Ernest Hemingway, James Joyce and Gertrude Stein.*

F. Scott Fitzgerald was among the writers who socialized with the staff of the Trib. *He once drunkenly commandeered an editor's desk in the newsroom and declared it was time to publish the paper. Another time he announced he had just been to a particular brothel and recommended it highly.*

CHAPTER 13
To Poland, Russia and Timbuktu

As the man handing out the assignments, Gibbons was always sure to give himself choice ones, even if they were seemingly impossible. One of these came in 1920 when he bluffed his way into Poland during the Polish-Russian War to interview the Polish Army Chief of Staff. The countries were battling over control of what are now Belarus and Ukraine, with the Russians hoping to create a border with Germany so they could pursue a communist revolution there. Reporters were banned from the front, but Gibbons had a plan.

He scraped together all the medals he had been awarded or could find, including one for a dog show—in case anyone missed the point. When Gibbons met the chief of staff, the officer eyed the impressive metallic array, clicked his heels, snapped a salute and asked anxiously how he could help the American visitor. Gibbons returned the salute and demanded: "I would like a military escort to the front right away." He got it, and for 47 days Gibbons was the only reporter present for the leading international news story of the period. The less ingenious correspondents were left to their thumb-sucking at the border awaiting news from second-hand sources. Gibbons had done it to them again.

Following Gibbons' coverage of the Russo-Polish conflict, he went to Russia to cover one of the most horrific famines in European history. World War I, the Communist revolution, war with Poland, plus a drought, had taken a severe toll on farming. A profound grain shortage resulted, and from the spring of 1921 through 1922 millions of Russians starved to death. Russia was not eager for the West to know of its troubles. But Gibbons chased the story relentlessly.

According to Sally Taylor, the author of *Stalin's Apologist: Walter Duranty*, Gibbons "had chartered a plane and told Russian leader Maxim Litvinov he planned to fly into Red Square in it, giving his paper a big

Gibbons on his way to the 1920 Polish-Russian conflict. He rarely missed an opportunity for self-promotion. This flight nearly ended in his death when one of the plane's guide wires connecting the wing snapped and tore into the plane's controls. The pilot crash-landed the Sopwith and pulled Gibbons from the wreckage. A second Sopwith sent to pick him up also crashed, almost killing its pilot.

scoop and Russian security a black eye. Appalled at the prospect, Litvinov instead offered Gibbons the chance to go early into the area stricken by famine, exactly what Gibbons had been after all along." Walter Duranty of *The New York Times* said that Gibbons "fully deserved his success because he had accomplished the feat of bluffing the redoubtable Litvinov stone-cold...a noble piece of work." Gibbons not only bluffed his way in, but also bluffed his means of getting the story back to Chicago. Before leaving for Russia, he wrote a fake telegram to be sent to himself saying the U.S. Senate was waiting for his report on pins and needles.

"There are things one would want to forget," wrote Gibbons, "that picture of living skeletons so close together they were almost piled upon one another—humans wrapped up in dirty gunny sacks and burlap; of scrawny hands reaching for bread; of naked babies with stomachs distended...men and women walking around in a daze...altogether, ten million people were starving to death in Russia." Gibbons helped spotlight the disaster and the U.S. sent shipload after shipload of food, eventually helping resolve the crisis.

Years later, a fellow journalist gave a poignant account of Gibbons' role in feeding a few of those millions. In a June 1942 *American Mercury* article, Helen Augur described how she and other reporters traveled with Gibbons by train and boat in Russia. "We had watched the great reporter come into Russia like a big game hunter and get his story. Yet we saw him licked and weeping, because now his quarry would pursue him for the rest of his life." Gibbons had taken control of the little traveling party and he got them to agree that since they could not feed all, they would feed none. Aboard a huge side-wheeler with a crew of 30, Gibbons and the others sailed up the Volga to further observe the horrors of starvation, illness and death. They found it left, right and center and Gibbons could stand it no more. He told his colleagues: "We're Americans, and it's our business to feed these people, and not make so many promises about boats that are just loading up now in New York. Let's get a little action here."

The reporters pooled their rubles and sent members of the boat crew to neighboring towns where precious bread was available, but for

Starving children during the 1921 Russian famine. Gibbons had bluffed his way into the heart of an area beset with famine and reported exclusively on it firsthand. The Polish-Russian conflict, Russian civil war and a drought contributed to the deaths of millions by starvation and disease.

exorbitant prices. They bought thirty loaves and as hundreds gathered only mothers and their children could be fed.

Crushed by their limitations, the journalists returned to their boat. Gibbons wept from "his hard china-blue eye" and cursed the fates that had condemned the Russians, according to the *Mercury* article: "Damn it," he roared finally, "they're no goddamned Boches. These people were our allies in the War."

Augur long held that Gibbons could only put that matter in "soldier-talk.... He suffered in the war, so he has put the suffering of the peasants in the biggest terms he knows. But his mind can't cross the trenches."

More than a decade later she found the news story he wrote that sad day, changing her view "in one labored, honest sentence."

> "We, who gave the bit of food, received more good from it than those who received it, because in a measure it atoned for the fact that we had in our bodies the warmth of ample food, and were wearing whole clothes, and were housed on a boat while 400 fellow-humans of our color and belief in our God were dying miserably within a stone's throw."

Gibbons used the novelty of each assignment to get over what pain the previous one had brought. His restlessness and love of travel and adventure helped him from being too introspective. Gibbons liked to come up with his own story ideas, but the Chicago bosses often thought theirs were better. Imagine Gibbons' incredulity when he got the following telegram:

February 1, 1923

GIBBONS

CHITRIB, PARIS

ORGANIZE AND EQUIP CAMEL CARAVAN CROSS
SAHARA DESERT OBTAIN TRUE PICTURE SHEIKS AND
THEIR APPEAL ANGLO SAXON AND AMERICAN
WOMEN...WIDE   INTEREST   HERE   [in]   RUDOLPH
VALENTINO'S CHARCTERIZATION IN MOVIES CABLE
WHEN CAN LEAVE.

Gibbons jumped to plot a 2,000 mile trip across the Sahara from
Columb Bechar, Algeria, to Timbuktu, Upper Senegal, that would transit
from one Foreign Legion outpost to the next. Gibbons was told by the
Foreign Legion that even the most experienced travelers would need four
months to complete the journey. The plucky Gibbons said he'd do it in
two. The correspondent engaged 24 soldiers and camel drivers to make
the trip, and armed with all possible supplies (including several of his
mother's lipsticks to fend off the sun), they took off carrying American
and French flags. The caravan traveled largely by night to avoid the
scalding sun and heat. Amid numerous sand storms, Gibbons had his men
hold onto their camel's tails as he led his own by its reins. Illness too
struck the caravan, and Gibbons was once forced to amputate part of a
man's foot.

The caravan came upon a village that had just been ransacked by
slavers, who had stolen six children to be sold off. The villagers had
captured one of the raiders and were about to kill him. Gibbons talked
them into allowing him to take the prisoner to the authorities, which he
did.

Gibbons completed his eastward trip on July 1, 1923, arriving in
Timbuktu, a little over three months after he began. Years before, a
Minneapolis editor had fired him by telling him angrily to "go to
Timbuktu." Gibbons cheekily sent the man a postcard saying he had
arrived as told. And, unfortunately for his Chicago editors, the assignment
never yielded a single handsome romantic sheik. Said Gibbons: "(T)hey
are very unromantic." What it did yield, however, was the French Legion
of Honor from Marshal Ferdinand Foch, the Jesuit-trained soldier who led
French forces against the Germans in WW I. The Award was given for
upholding French ideals while crossing the desert with French and
American colors.

Gibbons in his Sahara garb. The Tribune *in 1923 assigned Gibbons to head a 2,000-mile expedition across the Sahara to find the true nature of the Arab sheik. Rudolph Valentino's role as one on the screen had created a mania in the states and the* Trib *hoped to explore it. Gibbons encountered slavers, illness and severe conditions. The French Foreign Legion told Gibbons not to attempt the crossing during the summer, but he did, completing it in three months, rather than the Legion's estimate of four. The caravan carried American and French flags, and the French awarded Gibbons the Legion of Honor for doing so.*

The Sahara trip was one of many such expeditions and travel stories that reporters and adventurers of all stripes attempted during the '20s. As American doughboys returned to the states, they had seen for the first time that there were worlds quite apart from their farms, villages and factories and they were eager for more. Movies, early radio and newspapers saw that the public's appetite for this information was strong and attempted to meet it.

While such trips seemed romantic, the realities were often painful. Writing from Lagos, Nigeria, in 1923 during a river expedition, Gibbons told brother, Ed: "You have no idea how damned lonesome it gets down here.... I have to keep doped up with quinine all the time—ears constantly ringing with it. I am much fatter than I left Paris but very soft on account of fact that white men can't exercise in this heat. We are even carried through the streets in hammocks instead of walking. Just sitting here typing this makes sweat run and this coupled with prickly heat and all kinds of insect bites makes life a continual torture."

Gibbons returned to Chicago in July 24 after a five-year absence from the states. His parents and brother Ed had moved to be near him in Paris previously and he saw little need to return stateside, but Izzy now seemed ready to divorce after months of stalling. Their marriage ended on August 24, 1924, after 10 years including two years of formal separation.

Now other big changes were in store for Gibbons.

The Chicago Tribune's trans-Sahara expedition has reached its goal after a series of exciting experiences. Map shows route pursued by Floyd Gibbons and his party across northern Africa, from the Mediterranean to the Atlantic.

CHAPTER 14
A New Outlet—Radio

Gibbons returned again to Chicago at Christmas 1925. His mother, Emma, had died after bladder surgery in Paris on Nov. 14, and Gibbons' father and brother, Edward, joined him in making the sad Atlantic trip for burial in Washington, D.C. Gibbons was in Rome interviewing leaders of the fascist movement Nov. 12 when his mother took her final turn for the worst. Gibbons tried to arrive bedside for a last good-bye, but he failed, leaving him devastated. His mother had been in a Paris hospital for several weeks while he was in Rome and he first heard of the crisis state in a telegram from his brother Edward Nov. 12. Gibbons had jumped aboard the next Rome-Paris Express for the 36-hour trip after being unable to charter a plane. He arrived 18 hours too late to say adieu to Emma.

Gibbons sailed with his family from France on Dec. 15, the earliest they were allowed to leave because of paperwork required to transport a body to the States.

Shortly before Christmas and after a funeral mass at the tony St. Thomas the Apostle Church in Washington, D.C., the family buried its matriarch at Mt. Olivet Cemetery on Bladensburg Road NE. Gawler's, the long-established Catholic funeral home with Gonzaga connections, handled the arrangements.

Gibbons left almost immediately for Chicago, where members of the overseas staff were expected to return when possible to reacquaint themselves with the paper's corporate and editorial culture and to touch base with its Midwestern roots. Gibbons no doubt was eager to use the visit to see how best to promote the Gibbons brand.

Since his last trip home, the *Tribune* empire had gotten deeper into a new medium that seemed pure Gibbons: radio. The war had stalled pioneering experiments with the technology before they could develop commercially, but with the Armistice the radio floodgates opened.

Floyd Gibbons, far right; brother Edward, middle; father Edward, far left, aboard a ship.

A home radio receiver in 1926 cost about $125, counting antenna, batteries and headset, the equivalent of $1,500 today. But consumers were head-over-heels in love, and within two years of KDKA Pittsburgh's first non-experimental scheduled broadcast of Presidential election results on Nov. 2, 1920, some 1.2 million radios were in use. American homes tuned to some 550 stations, at least one in each state. The government assigned station call letters from a list created for maritime radio use. The K meant a ship that plied the Atlantic or Gulf of Mexico while the W was reserved for Great Lakes ships. Their assignment, after a tortuous route, eventually came to mean K was used for western stations and W for eastern ones. A number of grandfathered anomalies exist.

Pittsburgh's KDKA and WWJ in Detroit were on the air many hours a day; the *Detroit News*, which owned WWJ, stacked its transmitter atop its new building at 615 West Lafayette Blvd. and then stretched an aerial 290 feet to the roof of the Hotel Ft. Shelby. KDKA and WWJ programmed debates, opera, boxing, college football and professional baseball games, some prerecorded. Initially, hours for these and other stations were typically 10 a.m. to 7 p.m. Stations began to sell advertisers blocks of time that they could program as they liked, begetting shows like the Philco Hour, which featured prominent opera singers and its own orchestra, and the Wrigley Revue, which interspersed music and chat with paeans to chewing gum.

The *Tribune* had jumped into the new form with both feet, finagling for its flagship station the call letters WGN—World's Greatest Newspaper—gaining them from the owners of a ship they had graced. As counterparts around the country were doing, the station debuted with an array of recorded and live music, readings, debates and sports broadcasting. Programming originated from the Edgewater Beach Hotel, between Sheridan Road and Lake Michigan at Berwyn Avenue. The first programming for listeners aired from 6 p.m. Saturday March 24, 1924, to 8 a.m. Sunday. A *Tribune* survey that year found 100,000 Chicago residents had radios.

Gibbons took to his radio debut with the same elan and timing that marked his newspapering. He had left Washington by train Dec. 23. He took a cab straight from the train station to the *Tribune* the next morning. In the lobby coincidentally stood Quin Ryan, WGN station manager and chief announcer. Gibbons' visage and white eye patch were unmistakable, and Ryan hoped to work the newspaper's star reporter into the new medium, converting thousands of subscribers who knew the Gibbons byline into fans of the Gibbons voice (to listen, visit http://www.otr.com/gibbons.shtml and click on "Flooding in New England").

Ryan proposed that Gibbons come into the studio the next evening and tell listeners of places he had spent past Christmases. In print, Gibbons came across as a man's man and was catnip for women. He had vaulted from local and regional notoriety as a newsman to become an internationally known war correspondent—wounded in action, plucky, lucky, talented, and the very image of America as America saw itself in the mid-1920s. A relentless self-promoter, Gibbons felt the microphone's draw. The next day Gibbons arrived two hours early at the studio now in the Drake Hotel on East Walton Street. Uncharacteristically anxious, the war correspondent got a primer on broadcasting from Ryan, who described his protégé as "the most pliable of pupils." Ryan said later that Gibbons had been sensational. "He brought sincerity, genuineness and a colorful story telling ability that the radio listeners had never known before," the broadcaster said. The station and the newspaper were so pleased with that result they had Gibbons become one of the first multimedia correspondents. He would write an article for the *Trib*, broadcast it, and listeners and readers were asked which they preferred. They invariably liked the broadcasts better.

Ryan and his colleagues at WGN wanted to keep Gibbons on the air in Chicago, but *Tribune* management in January 1926 sent him back to Europe. Newspapering at home or abroad was a more certain conduit of revenue than radio. But before Gibbons set sail, the *Trib* had him go to Washington for a stunt and possible scoop on behalf of WGN. The man who had survived a mid-Atlantic torpedoing, German machine gunners, and the rigors of a trans-Sahara trek took on the ultimate challenge: Make President Calvin "Silent Cal" Coolidge interesting to radio listeners.

Coolidge took a daily constitutional in the vicinity of the White House; Gibbons got the okay to tag along a chilly Jan. 27.

"The appointment was made for five o'clock in the evening. I was there fifteen minutes early" Gibbons told his audience. "The President did not emerge from his office until five forty-five. He joined me without a word, buttoning up his overcoat. We were followed by two detectives. We walked two blocks before either of us said anything. I was trying to think of what subject would interest him. Finally he said, 'Nice crispy weather.' So I tried to bring up some of my experiences by countering with, 'Yes, but it doesn't agree with me. My blood is thin from my sojourn in Africa.'

"The President digested this in silence, and then came a three-word question: 'You in Morocco?'

'Yes.'

'How long and when?'

"I replied briefly and the President asked, 'How are airplanes used in the war there?'

"This called for a reply of some length. Then we walked for many blocks in silence. The only time he stopped was when we were passing a photographer's window filled with photographs of familiar statesmen.

"The only other words addressed to me by the President were these: 'Been in Siberia? How long and when?'

"Then he invited me to breakfast the following morning, and what a good old-fashioned breakfast it was—wheatcakes, sausage, and New England syrup."

Even Gibbons could not make Coolidge sound more interesting than breakfast.

Gibbons did say, however, that his most exciting moment of the stroll came when Coolidge grabbed his arm to keep him from the path of an oncoming cab.

A Washington stroll with President Calvin Coolidge was the subject of one of Gibbons' earliest broadcasts in January of 1926. Even the glib Gibbons couldn't get much out of the man known as Silent Cal.

Gibbons was a very early broadcast experimenter. Here he does a remote spot broadcast of the departure of the Graf Zeppelin *from Lakehurst, N.J., in Aug. 1929. He used a 24-pound transmitter originally designed by NBC for a parachute broadcast. He also broadcast from trains and ships.*

Sailing back to Europe, Gibbons had time to absorb his brief taste of radio. The experience brought out an unusual anxiety that he addressed in a letter to Quin Ryan.

"You asked me what I think of radio," Gibbons wrote. "I am beyond thinking. I am blubbering. I am stumped. I've seen a few strange places and tingled to a few unique sensations, but nothing has left me so completely flabbergasted as that little shining instrument on the desk in the WGN studio."

He said when broadcasting his throat went dry, his face flushed and his palms sweated. Only scribbling hard with a pencil allowed him to maintain his concentration, he said. Even so, Gibbons told his colleague, he was grateful to WGN for the chance "to feel real humanity through a new medium." Though the station had received hundreds of fan letters praising Gibbons, he doubted his broadcasting aptitude.

That would change.

CHAPTER 15
The Red Baron and 'The Red Napoleon'

Gibbons' Sahara and Niger river trips and unsuccessful pitches for a North Pole flight and an Amazon trek had whetted his entrepreneurial bent, and he craved to do something else. It had been too long since the excitement of the Mexican incursion, the drama of the *Laconia* sinking and his wounding at Belleau Wood. At age 39 in 1926, Floyd Gibbons was wondering again what the world had in store for him.

"I want to take a fling at the magazine game and I know I can deliver," he had written Irvin Cobb of the *Saturday Evening Post*, a colleague when covering the Great War. He hoped Cobb could help him reinvent himself stateside. In Europe, Gibbons was making $12,000 per year ($163,000 in current dollars) plus a small share of the *Paris Tribune* profits "which are not considerable." The *Tribune* "treats me well and I can probably stay at the head of their foreign field forever but I dread getting into the rut of an expatriate," Gibbons told his fellow writer who was famous as a humorist.

Gibbons attempted to sell himself to Cobb by noting he had some 20 million daily readers and that *And They Thought We Wouldn't Fight* sold 35,000 copies. Gibbons closed the letter whimsically: "I sincerely trust that the doctors have taken nothing away from you since your last inventory and that the supply pump on your cocktail shaker is in good working order. When you get through wearing Mark Twain's mantle as a vest, I'd like to rent it for a tent."

Gibbons' fatigue with the *Tribune*, unbeknownst to him, was a two-way street. While perusing his mail at a Bucharest café some months after the Chicago visit, he discovered he'd been fired. He had worked there for 15 years. Notes from his brother Edward say he was never told the reason for the firing. Speculated his brother in a note: "It couldn't have been inefficiency, because the *Tribune* had given him a large bonus only the year before." Salvation came in the form of Joseph Medill Patterson, co-publisher of the *Chicago Tribune* and publisher of the *New York Daily News*, who hired Gibbons to write a series for *Liberty Magazine*, to be turned into a book. Gibbons was to write about Baron Manfred von Richtofen, the German ace, who was known as the Red Knight because of the color of his plane. (Cartoonist Charles Schultz dubbed him the Red Baron and made him more famous than Gibbons' book ever could have.)

The Red Knight is a superb piece of reporting and meticulous research, taking a year to complete and documenting all of the Baron's victories and his single, final loss. Liberty serialized the book for 23 consecutive weeks, an unusually long run.

Patterson was so happy with *The Red Knight* that he asked Gibbons to write a novel in 1929 imagining the next world war. *The Red Napoleon* told the story of a Russian dictator who tried to take over the world and attempted to meld all races. It too was serialized the same year and published as a book. Gibbons personally asked Leon Trotsky, the expelled Russian revolutionary, to write the book's introduction. Trotsky said yes, but it never happened.

The Red Napoleon, despite being characterized as pulp fiction, was reprinted in 1976 in a Lost American Fiction series that described it as having "languished with an underground reputation." In the new edition's afterword, English Professor John Gardner of Southern Illinois University hails Gibbons' novel as a "landmark that slipped by unnoticed... the work of a visionary and satirist in the tradition of Defoe." The cover blurb trumpets "Gibbons' social vision includes bloodshed in east Asia and the expulsion of the French, the beginning of the second World War with a lightning strike into Poland, the unification of China...the Wall Street crash and worldwide depression, and the astonishing prediction of the rise of the Third World."

Far less complimentary was the Nov. 21, 2012, issue of *Foreign Policy* which reviewed the book in comparison with the remake of the *Red Dawn* movie about a Cuban-Soviet invasion of the U.S. Writer J.M. Berger missed any satire and described the book as "stuffed with perfervid nationalism and over-the-top racism beyond the wildest dreams of anyone working in Hollywood today." Berger wrote that "while *The Red Napoleon* is far more overtly political than its *Red Dawn* descendants, it's not much more subtle or complex. Lefties, pacifists, and dirty foreigners are the problem, righties and whiteys are the solution."

English professor Gardner noted in 1976 that Gibbons predicted that anti-Semitism would contribute to a world war, though Gibbons thought from Russia, not Germany.

Germany, however, was itself frightened of Gibbons and other writers. As early as 1930, Gibbons saw Hitler for what he was, and condemned him. The Germans in turn considered Gibbons' and others' books "harmful and undesired," according to the *Faulkner Journal*, putting him in the company of Hemingway, Sinclair Lewis and other famed authors on the Reich's banned list.

While Gibbons' politics may have put him in the same ranks as these great writers for Nazi purposes, as a writer he was hardly their equal. His prose in *Red Napoleon* is often cliché-ridden and filled with stereotypes. This was magazine writing converted to a book and designed for mass appeal, an appeal far less sophisticated in style than the decades that have followed. Gibbons had honed his writing style at the *Tribune*, where he told a fellow foreign correspondent: "You must always write down---don't be 'intellectual,' the people who buy the *Tribune* in Chicago don't understand or give a damn about Far Eastern politics—they want hot stories about battle and bandits."

Gibbons' penchant in broadcasts and in *Red Napoleon* to make himself the chief protagonist rankled some journalists, but his sister saw this as a natural professional extension. "Floyd was a dazzlingly successful journalist," said his sister Zelda Mayer in a 1956 letter to a graduate student, "but like most other persons who make good in their work, he aspired to even greater accomplishments... So he used *The Red Napoleon* as a medium for a vicarious wish-fulfillment, in which he portrayed himself as sitting alone in a front-row seat at all of the world changing events, receiving confidences from the world's leaders, and sending back exclusive dispatches...who is to say such dreaming was censurable."

Vanity Fair was a critic of Gibbons for continually writing and broadcasting about conflict. "[I]n 25 years of public battening on war he has always forgone the opportunity to mold public opinion towards peace, preferring to see war as a 'show'; because he is a professional hero, patriot and jingoist; because he recently continued his headline hunting at Shanghai, where he again exploited human tragedy." The magazine included Gibbons on a list with Hitler of people it wished would just "go away." *Vanity Fair* published a caricature of Gibbons by famed artist Miguel Covarrubias showing Gibbons, his single eye flaring, typing in the midst of battle. His typewriter keys say simply: "Oh Boy!"

Literary Digest magazine in 1932 had a different view. "Mr. Gibbons is notorious...for the integrity of his dispatches," it said, "...it is his passionate creed to report the doings of the universe aright, consecrated to accuracy and the abhorrence of radioed or cabled falsehoods. It may be in his weakness at times to overdress the naked truth in dramatic embroideries, and to make his own role in the comic pageant the principal one. Nevertheless his words are never altogether unreliable."

Gibbons saw his role through the words of his reporter character in *Red Napoleon:*

> "As the dramatic critic attends first nights and takes each new stage play through the agony of its first public appearance, so it has been my job to be present and observe the human strife and agonies, the bloodshed and misery, the maiming and torture, the burning and devastation of these recurring spasms and convulsions, which are the curse of mankind.

> "I could not compute the hundreds of men I had actually seen killed—shot—burned—blown to bits. I would not figure the thousands I had seen dead on the fields and streets of battle. I hated to total the tens of thousands of maimed and wounded, of blinded and crippled, I had seen in war time hospitals around the world. I avoided estimating the hundreds of thousands, if not millions, of war victims,

living and dead, I had written about during my years as a war correspondent from 1914 to 1928."

An article in *American Mercury* in Jan. of 1933 by Henry Pringle disputes *Vanity Fair*'s view of Gibbons as war lover, saying Gibbons can no more be blamed for his role than a defense counsel can be in a criminal trial. But the *Mercury* piled on anyways. One time period, it described as "happy days. Carnage raged throughout the world and Mr. Gibbons had only to choose which war to cover."

With World War I, Gibbons had a great stage, Pringle said, and his fellow reporters resented him continually looking like he was awaiting his cue for the spotlight.

"He seemed to have an inside track everywhere. His uniform was the snappiest in London or Paris. He darted in and out of American headquarters and was often saluted by mistake. He swept down the boulevards in an enormous army car, a daily occurrence which was the greatest of irritants…He seemed to be very much in the confidence of the mighty. He careened along, if only to mail an expense account, as though Pershing, Foch and all the other brass hats were waiting for him to endorse their plans to stop the thrust of the German armies."

Nor did Pringle have much sympathy for Gibbons' war wounds. He called his eye patch "a valuable trademark, like the Victrola dog."

Though not trademarked, Gibbons' newsman character in *Red Napoleon* does report by means unique at the time, broadcasting while moving from such places as airplanes and battleships. To learn more about field broadcasting for the book, Gibbons interviewed the brass at the NBC radio network, including network President M. H. Aylesworth. Gibbons was nothing if not ambitious and certainly had other motives in chatting with the NBC executives. NBC saw what WGN had seen and offered Gibbons a New York-based national show, *The Headline Hunter*, sponsored by General Electric and begun in July of 1929.

Gibbons had overcome his doubts about radio and this time took to it as if performing on the stage his father built for him as a child. It seemed made for him. The spark and charm the Jesuits had seen in young Floyd Gibbons finally had its national audience. His delivery was unique and unmistakable. He was said to be the fastest talker on radio, rattling off 217 words per minute, 3.6 per second. Somebody called him "the fastest thing on spiels." And evidently, the speed, drama and news that he delivered were just what the American public wanted because the show and his popularity soared. Millions tuned into the weekly *Headline Hunter* with Gibbons' tales of covering the world and then an additional weekly show, *General Electric's Adventures in Science*, where Gibbons popularized scientific matters.

Within months of his first NBC national broadcast, he was receiving 1,000 letters a week, including missives from fans General Pershing, Will Rogers and his own Aunt Til. The Post Office began delivering letters to him addressed only with a sketch of a man wearing an eye patch. His fame spread so quickly and thoroughly he was invited to sail on Vanderbilt yachts, greet returning explorers and tamp down a spate of Gibbons imposters pushing various scams. His favorite meal of creamed chipped beef on toast, with a dessert of figs, became newsworthy. Whenever he dined out, inevitably a former Marine would approach and recount how he was the one who had helped save Gibbons on the battlefield. Some actually believed it, and Gibbons never failed to buy each a drink. One thousand letters per week quickly became a thousand a day. Even reporters were smitten. *Washington Post* radio columnist Robert Heinl wrote Nov. 10, 1929 that Gibbons' "powers of observation, his ability to speak as well as he writes, his enthusiasm, and the tremendous following would be a great ballyhoo for anything...."

Pringle of the *American Mercury*, certainly confirming the views of the magazine's curmudgeonly intellectual editor, H. L. Mencken, saw Gibbons' success stemming from a "a great psychological truth. This was that it is quite impossible to underestimate the public taste or mass appetite for the silly. He discovered that he was speaking to an audience on an even lower level than that of a motion picture." This same audience, however, found Gibbons "a pleasing relief from the treacle which clogged the radio channels, from the honeyed tones of announcers, from the crooners and whiners," Pringle wrote. *Time* magazine was never a Gibbons fan. It repeatedly faulted his "breathless" reporting and called his reporting language "Gibbonish." In 1935, it called Gibbons a "trained seal" and mocked his "Hello, Everybody" trademark opening line. And it noted Gibbons used the word "I" at the rate of "five times per sentence." Another time it described him as "garrulous, hysterical and frequently absurd."

If Gibbons was bothered by the criticisms, he never let on and certainly never changed his style.

CHAPTER 16
With Hoover in His Hideaway

Radio's power to inform and persuade attracted politicians. Herbert Hoover had regulated radio as commerce secretary and early on saw its advantages. Now, as president, he spent a remarkable August 1930 weekend with Gibbons at Hoover's Virginia hideaway on the eastern slopes of the Blue Ridge Mountains where two streams join to form the Rapidan River. Gibbons' 28-page broadcast script tries hard to personalize Herbert Hoover, whom Gibbons clearly admired. And the President certainly became more human when he loaned Gibbons his own belt, his own hat and a car to get him to a train on time.

"He looked up when he saw me coming," said Gibbons in his broadcast. "'Hello, Floyd,' he said, 'sit down.'…And as we talked, I began to wonder how many people…knew that his voice is quiet; that he speaks slowly; how many people know that he wears black socks with white shoes, and smokes a pipe with the preoccupied expertness of an old-time pipe-smoker."

After their short morning chat, Hoover suggested Gibbons may want to change clothes after the three-hour drive from Washington. It was then that Gibbons discovered he had not brought a belt for some outsized pants. Fortunately, Hoover's valet was nearby and resolved the problem—with the president's own spare. Gibbons' broadcast describes the president's plain former barracks built by the Marines. The accommodations were rustic and the luncheon meal—served on the ground picnic style—was far from grand.

After lunch, Gibbons and Hoover went on a hike. "The President led the way, and I was amazed at the agility of the man. He leaped from rock to rock…. For though he's the chief executive now, he's still an engineer –a prospector – at heart. There's nothing he likes better than to get into old clothes and potter around the rocks and stones."

President Herbert Hoover and wife Lou at Rapidan River retreat in Virginia. Gibbons spent a weekend with the couple there for a broadcast story in August 1930. He was clearly impressed with Hoover's intelligence and character. Gibbons had previously met with him in the White House on July 25, 1929.

Gibbons was bowled over by Hoover's intelligence and knowledge. "I've known two other Presidents [Wilson and Coolidge in office]. I've talked with both of them. But neither of them, as far as I know, or as far as I can conceive, ever had the wide grasp of affairs that President Hoover shows in the course of even the most casual chat.... He's a regular encyclopedia of everything that bears on the welfare of the country. He's got it all at his fingertips. No referring to secretaries – no pondering – no guessing. He knows."

Gibbons likely had landed the interview by promising not to quote Hoover and to do a profile rather than a hard-news piece. If the previous October's market crash and the looming depression came up, they didn't make it into Gibbons' story.

Gibbons said Hoover could make people feel comfortable with him "just by being comfortable with himself." The same was true with Mrs. Hoover, who happily gave Gibbons permission to use his hands to eat a fried chicken dinner served them on a plain pine table.

As the presidential party prepared to drive back to Washington, Gibbons couldn't find his $40 Panama hat. One of Hoover's aides spotted the dilemma and produced a solution, giving Gibbons the President's own sweat-stained floppy-brimmed Panama, complete with the $8 price tag in the head band. Said Gibbons: "I felt prouder in that hat than a fourteen-year-old kid in his first pair of long pants."

Only Gibbons had stayed with the Hoovers in camp. Other reporters observed the goings-on at a distance, and Gibbons rejoined them in the press car when their caravan gathered to depart. In saying goodbye, Hoover asked Gibbons what time his train was. Gibbons thought nothing of that until hours later near the Washington monument, when the convoy—against all security procedures—stopped abruptly and the newsmen saw Secret Service, police and aides scurrying to confer with the president's vehicle. Hoover had stopped the cars to direct police to escort the press car to Union Station so Gibbons would catch his train to New York.

Working during breakfast at the Mayflower Hotel on April 20, 1932, Gibbons prepares for a White House meeting with President Herbert Hoover to brief him on the conflict between Japan and Russia after the journalist's trip to the Far East.

Gibbons, left, and Bonus Army head Walter Waters address some of the 43,000 marchers to Washington in spring and summer of 1932. World War I vets had been given bonus certificates that could be cashed only in 1945. The marchers, including 17,000 veterans, demanded they be cashed immediately because of the Great Depression. The marchers erected shanties to live in near the Anacostia River, and President Hoover ordered the Army to remove them. After the buildings were torched, Gibbons publicly tangled with War Secretary Patrick Hurley, who said the fires were set by the marchers, not the Army. Gibbons had personally seen otherwise and said so.

Bonus marchers on the Capitol grounds.

CHAPTER 17
Floyd Gibbons, Inc.

Gibbons was as much a self-promoter as he was a journalist.

A possibly self-authored 1929 brochure touting himself for paid speaking engagements set the tone for ballyhooing his one-man show for years to come. The illustrated four-page pamphlet's cover bears a Harris and Ewing photo Gibbons had shot at the firm's 1313 F Street NW Washington studio. Gibbons appears serious and resolute, but a twinkle in his one eye hints at another side. The copy inside paints him as a "world adventurer and journalist." Photos within present him as wounded war correspondent, wearing a kuffiyeh and in a bespoke three-piece dark suit, handsome and debonair, but clearly a man of action—Indiana Jones as international reporter.

"His spiritual blood pressure is high; he must see life wherever it is running with the full turbulent current amid wars and rumors of wars," the highly Gibbonesque copy reads. "Or, if these are not available, the imperious urge of his nature drives him to those exotic regions where men live on the dangerous edge of life, where they grasp like wolves for the primal necessities and where strange and irrational codes of conduct throw life into high relief."

So successful was Gibbons as a broadcaster and self-promoter that he leveraged his *Headline Hunter* and GE shows to broadcast the first daily news program, a Feb. 24, 1930, NBC effort sponsored by *Literary Digest.*

Gibbons had reached the pinnacle of newscasting, but from the first Gibbons' lifestyle clashed with his sponsor. Since 1919 alcohol was banned through the Volstead Act, and *Literary Digest* publisher T. J. Cuddihy was a teetotaler. Gibbons made no bones during staff meetings about having been on "toots" and enduring their aftermaths in the form of hangovers. Worse, according to broadcaster John Rayburn, he and his companions one riotous evening decided nothing would do at 2 a.m. but to roll out to Long Island and stop at Cuddihy's for a nightcap. *Literary Digest* promptly gave Gibbons and NBC the boot, taking its daily news program and sponsorship to the Columbia Broadcasting System and the sober-sided Lowell Thomas, whose broadcast career would last into the 1970s.

If *Literary Digest* wanted to wash its hands of Gibbons, he found that GE and others were more than willing to give him a firm hand shake. With Gibbons as famous and popular as ever, GE turned his weekly half hour show into an hour program Saturday nights while Libbey-Owens-Ford glass continued to support his Sunday show for them. Meanwhile, he resumed the lucrative speaking circuit that had to be curtailed because of the daily broadcasts for *Literary Digest*.

Gibbons shoe-horned in scores of speaking engagements (making about $300 hourly, $4,100 in current dollars), broadcasting from local stations when he could not get back to New York. Listeners couldn't get enough of Gibbons' voice, which had a deep-throated urgency, making those beside their Philcos feel like they are there and need to take some action. The more radio exposure Gibbons enjoyed, the more Gibbons' listeners wanted. Fan mail flooded in. Parents were naming their sons after him, his brother wrote, while the unbalanced stalked him or imposters pretended to be him.

In August 1930, Robert M. McBride and Company brought out *Floyd Gibbons: Knight of the Air*, an authorized biography of the 43-year-old reporter that so mythologized its subject that in Burton Rascoe's introduction, Gibbons himself cracked that he was scared he was "beginning to believe" his own press clips.

Gibbons' reputation as a man's man was part of his appeal, according to Rascoe, calling his subject's virility "simple, honest, direct, homely and ingenuous. And those are qualities that are somehow typical of America." Rascoe numbered among other of Gibbons' characteristics a dynamism and optimism, particularly appealing to a Depression-era America needing hope that energy and industry would see the country through. Gibbons embodied the traits extolled by Norman Vincent Peale, whose positive thinking philosophy the country had largely embraced.

A DAY IN THE LIFE OF FLOYD GIBBONS

6 A.M - AWAKENED BY TERRIFIC EXPLOSION OF BOMB OUTSIDE OF WINDOW

6.02 A.M BLOWN HIGH IN AIR LANDED ON AIRPLANE HEADED FOR GUADALOUPE ISLANDS

9.16 A.M. - CRASHED INTO MOUNTAIN IN FOG.

11.01 A.M. PICKED UP BY ROVING BAND OF BEDOUINS   HELD CAPTIVE

1. P.M. BRIBED BEDOUIN CHIEF, WAS RELEASED.

2.17 P.M. - BOARDED TRAMP SCHOONER BOUND FOR FORMOSA.

4.00 P.M. WRECKED BY TYPHOON OFF COAST OF MADAGASCAR

4.30 P.M. - BRAVED STORM-SWEPT SEA IN OPEN BOAT.

4.35 P.M. - SUCKED UP BY WATERSPOUT.

4.46 P.M. - DROPPED INTO DEEP JUNGLE SOMEWHERE NEAR AFRICAN GOLD COAST.

4.48 P.M. - CAPTURED BY CANNIBALS AND ESCAPED UNDER HEAVY FIRE.

5.00 P.M. - MANAGED TO GET TO OFFICE BY MOTORBOAT JUST IN TIME TO WRITE STORY FOR LAST EDITION.

Judge Magazine's *view of adventurer Gibbons in 1931.*

Another book, *Men of Daring*, illustrated by artist Stookie Allen, included Gibbons among 45 popular male figures of the day. Portraying Gibbons as "a fiction hero come to life" in two pages of drawings and text, Allen ranked the reporter alongside Charles Lindbergh, Buffalo Bill Cody, President Theodore Roosevelt and World War I hero T.E. Lawrence. Another in Allen's illustrated pantheon was "Fighting Bob" Evans, a naval hero of the Spanish-American War who, like Gibbons, had attended Washington's Gonzaga College High School.

Flogging the Gibbons story, press agents for NBC, General Electric and others fed *Photoplay* and *Radio Mirror* and other popular magazines detailed accounts of how Gibbons as a broadcaster relied on a particular routine: In the studio, he always sat on a straight-backed chair, wearing a fedora with the brim pulled down to protect his good eye from glare. He still carried a rabbit's foot for luck, a talisman given to him by an African witch doctor, which rode in a pocket of his vest. Just before going on the air, Gibbons would give the rabbit's foot a touch. He believed his fortunes were best when he wore a blue surge suit with a blue tie on a rainy day. He barred visitors from his studio as bad luck. Once the microphone went live, Gibbons was in his element. "Hello, everybody!" he would exclaim. In his right hand was the script he wrote, typed in jumbo type, seven words to a line and triple-spaced. Left out of these accounts was the fact that before each broadcast Gibbons took a heavy shot of booze to settle his nerves.

On the air he had help keeping himself in cigarettes. He smoked four packs a day, often Old Golds, and during the show the production manager had among his many duties the constant supplying and lighting of his boss's smokes a few feet from the No Smoking sign.

In 1937 a reporter for *Radio Mirror* trailed Gibbons to his Manhattan lair. "Floyd lives in a midtown hotel. His offices occupy two large suites, and he himself lives in a third," reporter Norton Russell wrote. "The office suites are bare and business like, filled with desks, filing cabinets, bundles of newspapers and scurrying secretaries. Floyd's own apartment is filled with mementos of countries he has visited, stories he has covered, an ash tray presented him at West Point, a cobweb soft shawl he bought in Spain, a glassed in colony of ants…. In place of honor, a portrait of Clarence

A FEW DAYS AFTER HIS OBITUARY WAS READ IN AMERICA A 4000-WORD STORY OF THE SINKING WAS RECEIVED BY HIS PAPER FROM IRELAND. HE HAD BEEN PICKED UP BY A BRITISH BOAT. THE STORY STIRRED UP GREAT INTEREST AND WAS READ ON THE FLOOR OF THE U.S. SENATE. 5 WEEKS LATER AMERICA DECLARED WAR. HE WAS THE FIRST OF THE CORRESPONDENTS TO ARRIVE IN FRANCE AND HE STAYED UNTIL THEY HAD TO CARRY HIM OUT. AT CHATEAU THIERRY HE LOST HIS LEFT EYE.

HE RECEIVED MANY MEDALS FROM THE FRENCH AND ITALIAN GOVERNMENTS. SINCE THE WAR HE HAS COVERED AT LEAST ONE REVOLUTION EVERY YEAR. 5 YEARS AGO HE WAS LOST WHILE LEADING AN EXPEDITION IN THE SAHARA DESERT. FOR 3 MONTHS HE PUSHED ON ACCROSS THE SWELTERING SAHARA UNTIL HE FINALLY REACHED TIMBUCTU AND SAFETY.

HE ALSO TREKKED 11,000 MILES THROUGH THE JUNGLES OF AFRICA. HE GATHERED NEWS IN THE BATTLE-SCARRED BALKANS AND REPORTED THE REVOLUTIONS IN RUSSIA. HE COVERED THE SPANISH-RIFF WAR AND ALMOST LOST HIS LIFE DURING A WILD MIX UP WITH RIFFIAN HORSEMEN. FOR MONTHS HE WAS LAID UP IN A HOSPITAL.

THE HEADLINE HUNTER HAS JUST RETURNED FROM CHINA WHERE HE COVERED THE RECENT FIGHTING BETWEEN CHINA AND JAPAN. WHERE HE WILL BE NEXT NO ONE KNOWS, BUT YOU CAN REST ASSURED IT WILL BE IN THE **HEART OF THE ACTION!**

Darrow." An earlier *Brooklyn Eagle* feature on the broadcaster had described an "Upper 40s" Manhattan apartment as filled with some 100 photos of himself and others at news events he covered. They competed for space on the crowded walls in the bedroom, living room and foyer. A half dozen typewriters sat about, as did two mysterious locked tin chests that reporter Mack Millar thought looked like treasure chests. Gibbons that day was dressed in a gray double breasted suit and matching hat, turned backwards. A white shirt, blue pin dot tie and brown shoes completed the look. "His sartorial make up was exceedingly smart," wrote Millar.

A *New York Daily News* feature on Gibbons made note of his "broad shoulders" and West Point-like walk. Reporter Alissa Keir in her 1931 column *Snapshots* described his face: "Square chin. Cluster of small moles under the left of it. Scar under the right of it, from a sock on the jaw. Irregular nose. Broken in a fight when he was ten. Muses over the occasion with relish. Says it was one grand fight. His own dog bit him on the fanny."

The article notes Gibbons "cusses lots. His vocabulary is the envy of every newspaperman. Must watch his step at the mike." On the religious side, fellow *Trib* correspondent George Seldes later wrote in *Witness to a Century* that Gibbons "went to Mass occasionally; he never mentioned going to confession, but he was certainly not anti-clerical." A letter from Gibbons to his father revealed a stronger spiritual sense, however. "… I share with you your great belief in God and the works of providence and I believe that his protection extends everywhere, irrespective of elements, heights or depths," he wrote. An ascetic, however, he was not.

His 1930 radio salary in today's dollars was $2.5 million while speaking gigs brought in hundreds of thousands more on top plus unknown income for endorsements. He'd come a long way from sleeping on Chicago park benches. But to get and stay there he needed to relentlessly pirouette among his roles as broadcaster, lecturer, and columnist—presaging the age of the personal brand. He endorsed everything under, and including, the sun as felt from the Crystal Pier Solarium in Santa Monica. ("I've taken nude baths all over the globe…but

I've never found the sun better than here in Santa Monica.") Cigarettes, socks, banks, movies and cars all drew his paid approval. He authorized a daily comic strip whose protagonist bore his name and started a correspondence school that enticed would-be Gibbonses to shell out to learn how Gibbons did his thing. Ads for the Floyd Gibbons School of Radio Broadcasting, headquartered in Washington, ran in outlets such as *Popular Mechanics.* The headline copy began with Gibbons' radio tag line "Hello, Everybody," followed by a pitch dangling "unlimited opportunities for men and women."

Gibbons' relentless hammering presence irritated some onlookers. Novelist Ernest Hemingway thought Gibbons' huckster instincts crass. The novelist, who declined even to prepare biographical information on himself for his own books, had his agent put out a statement generally blasting self-promotion by writers and citing Gibbons as an unwholesome example. "While Mr. H[emingway] appreciates the publicity attempt to build him into a glamorous personality like Floyd Gibbons or Tom Mix's horse Tony, he deprecates it and asks motion picture people to leave his life alone."

Other celebrity authors took kindly to Gibbons' efforts. Literary great Carl Sandburg, who knew Gibbons from their days together in Chicago newsrooms, enjoyed his former colleague's radio work. In a 1929 letter to Gibbons, Sandburg, who had received a Pulitzer Prize 10 years earlier for his poetry wrote: "Your voice is good and the mike and you are doing good team work...." A Gibbons story on the murder of a fellow correspondent by Pancho Villa's men helped inspire a poem, *Memoir of a Proud Boy,* in the book that won the Pulitzer, *Cornhuskers.*

Writer James Bellah in a 1956 letter to a graduate student said, "Floyd's genius flowered because there was nothing but (work) in his life. He arranged his life that way. A hotel-liver and a suitcase man, he was off at the sound of the first gun in any part of the world. His fallacy of life was undoubtedly that he never had anyone to bring his triumphs home to, except his editors."

Gibbons, as was the custom of the new radio medium, happily shilled for his advertisers on air, while lecturing and in his columns. But

Gibbons was becoming his own brand, launching a broadcasting school in 1931 and endorsing numerous products.

Poet Carl Sandburg praised Gibbons' broadcasting in a letter to him. The two had been Chicago newspapermen together earlier in their careers. Sandburg won the 1919 Pulitzer Prize for Poetry for his book Cornhuskers, *which included a poem about a fellow reporter murdered by Pancho Villa's men. It was inspired by a Gibbons story.*

Writer Ernest Hemingway and Gibbons in the Bahamas in 1936 aboard Hemingway's yacht Pilar. Hemingway thought Gibbons was too much of a self-promoter. (Corbis photo)

DeSoto advertisement.

even if they weren't radio advertisers, if the price was right, he would be happy to cover a product's story. Realsilk Hosiery brought him to its Indianapolis plant for a tour, resulting in a Gibbons byline atop an obvious advertisement in the *Saturday Evening Post* for the men's sock concern. De Soto paid him to write the copy for ads in the same magazine celebrating its 1932 models. Hoping to snare an Elgin watch endorsement fee, Gibbons proposed a first-person piece the company could use in an ad, but Elgin balked, twice asking to run the copy for nothing. By this time Gibbons knew his price and he stuck to it. "I am sorry to say that the answer to your letters of November 21st and January 15th is no," he wrote in 1937. "I write for a living and you make watches for a living. How the hell are either one of us going to live if we both start working for nothing, or am I crazy." Gibbons' eye for advertisers' interests went back to his early reporting days and once got him a gold-plated razor from Gillette. While interviewing former President Teddy Roosevelt as he shaved in 1912, he noticed Roosevelt was using the company's razor. He tipped off Gillette and the company sent their gilded thanks.

Gibbons' magpie brain led him into attempts at inventing products. Frustrated by losing shirt buttons, he patented a buttonless shirt he called chemise celibitaire, or "bachelor's shirt." Somehow the tie fastened the collar and narrow cuffs accommodated a wearer's hands.

As his father had, Gibbons sometimes dreamed too large. He and his brother Edward spent months planning a grand expedition that would have blazed a land route from Tierra del Fuego to Alaska. They imagined 30 vehicles and a team of 40, including technicians and scientists. Floyd and Edward eagerly buttonholed car makers and other prospects but the project sank under its own grandiosity. An undated to-do list of Gibbons' shows his Western Hemisphere Highway as the top priority, with a memo to be written on the subject for President Calvin Coolidge. Also on the list were a thousand-word treatment for movies based on his *Red Knight* book and another film called *Armageddon*, presumably based on *Red Napoleon*. (Neither film was made because Gibbons wouldn't give up radio rights.) Listed also were work on a school of Foreign Correspondents, a flight around the world and a design for a war map game.

Floyd Gibbons Confesses

How Famous War Correspondent Strayed from Fold and was Re-converted

Hello everybody: And make way, brothers, for a sinner. Confession is good for the soul. I was a barbarian taken into the fold, then a backslider that became lost in the wilderness and now stand here at the testimonial bench sincerely proclaiming my re-conversion.

Six presidential campaigns ago when Theodore Roosevelt was shot, I wrote a story about T. R. sitting on his hospital bed, placidly shaving with a Gillette razor, the while a would-be assassin's bullet was still imbedded in his shoulder.

The story won me my first safety razor. That first Gillette carried me through two rather tough bewhiskered campaigns in the Mexican revolution and was with me one night in 1917 when I was torpedoed in the North Atlantic. It still ought to be in Cabin 19 on the sunken Cunard liner *Laconia*, 200 miles off the Irish coast.

I landed in England with only a life preserver for baggage and in the rush to replenish toilet articles, a clerk in London sold me another kind of razor. I didn't like the substitute, but you know how people put up with anything in war time.

Well sir, I carried that chopper along with me through a series of wars all over the globe and even used it last year down in Africa when Mussolini's boys started their ruckus with Haile Selassie's subjects.

That hair puller was a hangover from world war days, proving that men are mostly creatures of habit and the habits are mostly bad. I had become accustomed to that scraper except for the fact that every year or so, I was forced to go beaver and grow a full crop of copper wire, simply to let my skin get back in shape.

Well sir, I'm reformed now. Several weeks ago I went through the Gillette plant in Boston and saw them turning out the new and up-to-date munitions of war for that every-morning conflict with man's greatest enemy, the stubbly chin.

I am back to the Gillette and the Gillette Blade after 19 years of dumb torture for which I have only myself to blame. I found the answer to painless shaves at the Gillette Safety Razor plant in Boston.

Here they take the world's finest steel, scientifically test and process it so that each blade is worth its weight in sheet platinum—worth more to me.

Apparently as much scientific care and skill are lavished on the Gillette Blade as in the production of a delicate spring for an astronomical chronometer.

And this blade is backed by years of experience, millions of dollars in research, and the reputation of an old-time pioneer organization, of which America can well be proud around the world.

Beavers of Habit, I give you Gillette.

Gibbons seemed to instinctively know how to market both himself and others' products.

Prototype for Gibbons' Headline Hunter *comic strip. Gibbons in the 1930s inspired comic book icon Stan Lee who had written him a letter and was shocked when Gibbons wrote him back. Lee had loved Gibbons' print and broadcast adventure stories and went on to become the most famous multimedia comic book creator in the country. Lee's first comic book script was called* Headline Hunter, Foreign Correspondent.

CHAPTER 18
Hollywood on the Hudson

Movies were as natural a progression for Floyd Gibbons as radio. The baritone Gibbons with his strong chin, slicked back black hair and remarkable eye patch seemed made for movies. Silent films had rendered actors with weak voices to unemployment lines and the sonorous types like Gibbons were in demand. First up for Gibbons was a short documentary on Woodrow Wilson released in 1931 called *The Big Decision*, but his most significant big screen experience came as narrator of the 1930 82-minute documentary *With Byrd at the South Pole*. The movie drew considerable attention and an Oscar for cinematography, the first Oscar ever for a documentary.

Gibbons also did a promotional talkie for the 1931 movie *Cimmaron*, an RKO big budget feature which won the first Best Picture Academy Award for a cowboy movie. In 1932, a *Film Daily* columnist reported Gibbons' agent had turned down $15,000 ($240,000 in current dollars) to act in a movie as a broadcasting war correspondent because he would be "stepping out of character." The dumbfounded columnist declared this the "first time such a sensational and revolutionary thing has happened in the history of show business." It's not clear whether this was for a role in the movie *War Correspondent* or the never-produced *The Life of Floyd Gibbons*. Given Gibbons' entrepreneurial streak, this report doesn't quite ring true, and in an age when columnists were more than happy to pass on rumors, it may not be true, or the role was rejected for other reasons, perhaps contractual.

War Correspondent featured a "craven poseur who romanticizes his newsgathering exploits hoping that his public will consider him a hero," *Time* magazine reported in 1932. And it said that if the main character had worn an eye patch "Gibbons might have good grounds for a libel suit."

Woodrow Wilson was the focus of Gibbons' first film work, shown here opening up at the Trenton, N.J., Trent Theater on Sept. 12, 1931.

With Byrd at the South Pole *was a big hit in 1930, with Gibbons doing the narration. The film won the first Oscar for a documentary for its cinematography.*

Gibbons' most prolific movie work came from a radio series he had hosted called *Your True Adventure.* In 1937, using that program as a model, Warner Bros. contracted with him to narrate and write shorts, brief films that rolled in movie houses before feature presentations, based on true adventure stories. Shot at New York's Vitaphone studio, the true adventure shorts used actors to portray the "heart stopping" events, often concluding with a cameo by the person who had survived the ordeal appearing in the final scene and introduced by Gibbons.

Gibbons made 26 true adventure shorts, produced between Sept. 18, 1937, and July 29, 1939. The films, which averaged 10 minutes in length, had titles like *Haunted House, Alibi Mark, Dear Old Dad, The Fighting Judge, Attic of Terror* and *Hit and Run.*

In 1938 he narrated a promotional trailer for Warner Brother's *The Adventures of Robin Hood*, starring Errol Flynn and Olivia De Havilland. About that time he worked on a short on eye health, a subject dear to his heart, called *Improved Vision.* In 1960, Hollywood recognized his narrative contributions on the Hollywood Walk of Fame, placing Gibbons' star between those of actor Robert Montgomery and producer Samuel Goldwyn at 1631 Vine Street. While not necessarily cooperating on movies about him, Gibbons had little issue with promoting others' films, presumably for a price. A *Film Daily* double-paged ad for *Little Lord Fauntleroy* in 1936 features Gibbons and other notables pushing the film. Said Gibbons, described as war correspondent and "soldier of fortune" in the advertising copy: *"Little Lord Fauntleroy* will grow up to be a real he-man, for he certainly is a he-boy. Maybe he'll be a war correspondent. My mother made me wear curls and a patent leather hat and it sure hardened me with the gang I traveled in." There was another movie he was not involved with but was likely actually about him. Called *Clear All Wires*, the 1933 MGM film starred Lee Tracy as a duplicitous, fast-talking, conniving foreign correspondent for the Chicago Globe. It was derived from a Broadway play by the same name, which was eventually reworked to appear as Cole Porter's hit musical *Leave it to Me* in 1938, starring Sophie Tucker and Mary Martin with Gene Kelly in his first Broadway dancing role. It had 307 performances and featured the still famous song "My Heart Belongs to Daddy."

The Adventures of Robin Hood *used Gibbons as an announcer for a trailer.*

Gibbons served as writer, announcer and characters in a series of shorts based on his broadcast listeners' experiences. Your True Adventures *came out in 1937 with titles like* Wanderlust, Defying Death, Hit and Run *and* Night Intruder.

By the late 1930s Gibbons had turned away entirely from radio to focus on movie work—though broadcasters continued to importune him with offers. One proposed a show called *Medals of Freedom* with Douglas Fairbanks Jr. In 1942, movie studios were eying Robert Preston or Don Ameche to play Gibbons in a proposed film *One Man Army*, which never got into production.

Gibbons' career had carried him far from the little neighborhood he'd grown up in in the nation's capital. He was not in Shaw anymore. Broadcasting and movie success in New York brought not only wealth and fame but a steady stream of invitations to opening nights, games, charity events, and an expanding circle of acquaintance with other denizens of celebrity Manhattan: boxer Jack Dempsey, Robert Ripley of *Believe It or Not* fame, and a batch of fellow journalists as prone as Gibbons to carousing. New York gossip writers like Walter Winchell, Heywood Broun and Damon Runyon made him a fixture in their columns. Apropos of his manly-man reputation and his insatiable curiosity, he became fascinated by fencing, attending competitions across New York and Connecticut, including the Outdoor Epee Championship of Connecticut, where Amelia Earhart handed out prizes. He loved horseback riding and rode through Central Park and Washington, D.C.'s Rock Creek Park when there.

Gibbons—or Gib as his friends called him— developed a taste for caviar and sometimes ate an entire tin with a spoon, all the while holding a lighted cigarette. Journalist James Bellah wrote in his 1947 *Irregular Gentlemen* of a three-day party that toggled between the Ambassador and the Barclay hotels, located several blocks apart in the eastside upper 40s of Manhattan. To enliven the festivities, Gibbons hired singers, jugglers and acrobats, and invited all his friends and relocated the rumpus from the Ambassador to the Barclay when, like a scene in a Marx Brothers comedy, the room overflowed. On another occasion, Gibbons herded a dozen visitors from his apartment, bearing bouquets and champagne, to Manhattan's St. Moritz Hotel to celebrate the birthday of aging Scottish soprano Mary Garden, known as the Sarah Bernhardt of Opera.

Gibbons' fame extended into the 1960s when ABC included The Floyd Gibbons Story *as an episode of* The Untouchables *on Dec. 11, 1962. Gibbons was played by Scott Brady, left, and lawman Eliot Ness by Robert Stack. The episode featured Gibbons investigating the murder of a fellow newsman by the mob. It served as a pilot for a proposed spin-off about Gibbons but it was never produced.*

In 1960, Hollywood recognized Gibbons' contributions on the Hollywood Walk of Fame, placing his star between those of actor Robert Montgomery and producer Samuel Goldwyn at 1631 Vine Street.

To Bellah, Gibbons was "that disquieting combination of a successful and fundamentally restless man so common in the United States in the twenties and thirties." Bellah said in *Irregular Gentlemen* the "tepid gruel" of celebrity could not nourish a man who really longed to be "the honest police reporter he had once been...."

Gibbons' money made that tepid gruel easier to swallow. He bought a 75-foot yacht, *The Adventurer*, which slept 10 and required a 3-man crew. The ship was built in 1920 for the equivalent today of $620,000 and rebuilt in 1937. Even though it had a 12-foot mahogany dinghy and a 14-foot power launch, Gibbons wanted something quicker and larger to get about. He bought a speedboat he named *Wham*, which he also used for forays into Long Island sound and up the Hudson. To go with his four-room penthouse in the Beaux Arts apartments on East 44th St. near Grand Central Station, he wanted something in a warmer clime. He settled on a waterfront residence in Miami Beach costing $25,000 ($500,000 today). But once his, the manse didn't do it for the peripatetic Gibbons. He spent only a matter of weeks actually occupying it.

While speaking and movies still drew top dollar, the war reporter in Gibbons longed to escape to the heady drama of combat. Italy's colonial ambitions in 1935 would serve as the springboard.

To see Gibbons at work, see the links below:

In 1931, Gibbons broadcast from Shanghai when the Japanese attacked China.

http://commerce.wazeedigital.com/license/clip/897001_469.do

Gibbons in 1934 taped a video of his predictions of life in 1959, a number of which were quite accurate.

http://mirc.sc.edu/islandora/object/usc%3A12352

CHAPTER 19
Last Call

Italian dictator Benito Mussolini in 1935 was preparing to invade Ethiopia, one of the last independent gems in Africa, as seen covetously under Mussolini's eyepiece. Italy controlled the countries north and south of Ethiopia—Eritrea and Somaliland—and the dictator planned to complete the domination of the region that Italy had attempted to do in the 1890s. Il Duce, as Mussolini was known, promised Italians a "place in the sun." With Marshal Emilio DeBono, Generals Rodolfo Graziano and Pietro Badoglio commanding some 700,000 troops, including 20 new divisions, Italy attacked from its northerly and southerly colonies on Oct. 3, 1935.

Some weeks earlier Gibbons was tasked by Hearst's International News Service with covering the invasion. On Saturday, Aug. 31 he sailed from New York to Naples, Italy, aboard the *S.S. Rex*. In Rome he met with Italian officials who flew him from Brindisi, Italy, to Asmara, Ethiopia. Gibbons not only talked the Italians into flying him across Ethiopia to view it from a large bomber, but he got Mussolini's son-in-law, Italian Press Minister Count Gian Galeazzo Ciano, to do the flying, giving Gibbons the rundown as they went. Gibbons flew over hundreds of square miles of the desert that was about to become part of the Italian empire. Gibbons wrote he wouldn't give one cent a square mile for the country, let alone fight for it.

The easy duty ended when Ciano, the eventual Prime Minister, set his bomber down back in Asmara. Gibbons, one of only two westerners initially covering the war, was no longer the young fit adventurer who had ridden with race car drivers and Mexican revolutionaries and trekked the Sahara. He was now 48 years old, burdened by his injuries from the Great War, and undone by a lifetime of smoking and drinking that had left him with heart disease. The daytime temperature in Ethiopia in October could reach 130 degrees Fahrenheit, and Gibbons often found himself at altitudes of as much as 8,000 feet. Bivouacking with troops in a war zone for two months meant sleeping badly, eating poorly, and enduring chronically unsanitary conditions. His weight dropped 40 pounds to 145. "I'm having a nervous breakdown!" *Time* quoted Gibbons as saying. According to the magazine, a photo of him in Ethiopia made him "unrecognizable...except for his trademark, the patch across one blind eye." Ever the game performer, however, Gibbons, working from a tiny town in Eritrea, wrote and transmitted by short wave radio a pair of reports that NBC picked up and distributed. As he was making the second broadcast he simply collapsed, probably from the heart disease. Gibbons was evacuated by plane to Khartoum, Sudan, on Oct. 26, where he rested four days before catching a train and boat to Cairo, which took an additional three days. After five weeks convalescence in Cairo, Gibbons went to Jerusalem to see the Holy City's sights and write of tensions between Muslims and Jews. When he was well enough, Gibbons returned to Rome.

There, Gibbons garnered interviews with Il Duce and Pope Pius XI—on the same day—some sort of record for yin and yang.

When Gibbons met with the cocky dictator, he hadn't formulated his first question, according to James Bellah's *Irregular Gentlemen*.

Gibbons walked towards Mussolini in his cavernous Palazzo Venezia office, with its 40-foot ceilings and 2,400 square feet of space. Faux marble columns adorned the walls. Behind the dictator rose a gigantic fireplace topped with a massive set of Fasces, bundled grain stalks and ax that symbolized the party. Gibbons approached the dictator and, as he did, Mussolini slapped his palm onto the top of his huge ornate wooden desk. "What do you want, Mr. Gibbons?" Il Duce barked, chin out like a pug.

"I don't want anything," Gibbons said, finally coming up with his question. "But one-hundred and forty-odd million Americans want to know what you are going to do in [Ethiopia]."

Mussolini took the bait, sat, and described in detail how he planned to colonize the African nation. But he also wanted information from

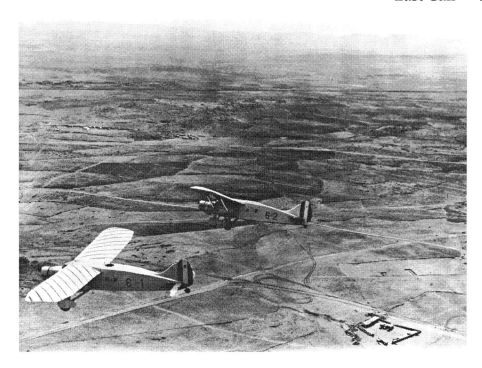

With typical flair, Gibbons not only talked the Italians into flying him across Ethiopia but also got Mussolini's son-in-law, Press Minister Count Gian Galeazzo Ciano, to do the flying. The count flew the Italian Air Force plane on the left. (Photo by Mondadori Portfolio via Getty Images)

Gibbons. He asked how his troops were doing. Evidently Gibbons did not hold them in high regard but dodged the query to keep Mussolini chatting. Mussolini seemed to be charmed by the American correspondent and even called him "Gibby."

Gibbons met Pope Pius XI, whose election he covered in 1922, in the Vatican, where he found him anxious about his next-door neighbor Mussolini and greatly interested in the Ethiopian war.

From Rome, Gibbons traveled through Paris to London on Jan. 21 where he covered the funeral of King George V. Uninterested in covering routine European news, Gibbons boarded the *S.S. Majestic* Feb. 13 and returned to New York six days later. Once back in the States, he was asked to brief President Roosevelt on the Ethiopian war and Mussolini. They met Wednesday, March 11, at 12:15, talking 15 minutes to a half hour.

*Italian dictator Benito Mussolini, whose invasion of Ethiopia
in 1935 brought Gibbons to cover that war. Gibbons returned
from the front and interviewed Mussolini, who first demanded
threateningly: "What do you want, Mr. Gibbons?" Said
Gibbons: "I don't want anything but one-hundred and forty-
odd million Americans want to know what are you going to do
in [Ethiopia]." Gibbons interviewed both Il Duce and Pope
Pius XI on the same day in Rome.*

Likely he was telling Roosevelt like he did his listeners that Italy would win in a walk. Gibbons had reported he found the dictator "filled with determination and conviction that his colonial venture will be a success. Mussolini was anything but worried when I saw him. He was the personification of confidence."

In the U.S., Gibbons resumed a routine of short-term broadcasting assignments, movie work and public appearances. In one he met his public relations match in J. Edgar Hoover, the fabled FBI chief. Hoover, an autocratic and peculiar man, carefully watched his own public image as the nation's watchdog against crime, subversion and sin. He was sure to cultivate Gibbons and even allowed him to try his hand on the FBI firing range. Gibbons held a gun permit in New York and had worked at his shooting since his Mexican Revolution days of pearl handled revolvers. On the range, a silhouette target flashed before him and he shot it cleanly 16 of 20 shots. J. Edgar autographed it and personally presented it. FBI men proudly showed Gibbons the group's fingerprint room and included Gibbons' prints among them—the 6,233,773rd to be taken. Hoover would later recall Gibbons as a "legend [with] matchless zeal and…candid humanity…."

Radio and other work were making him rich, but Gibbons was feeling stale, and when offered another war by Hearst's International News Service, Gibbons jumped again. On Aug. 8, 1936, Gibbons sailed from New York to Gibraltar aboard the S.S. Rex. His destination: Spain, to report on the revolution underway there led by the insurrectionist right wing General Francisco Franco against the leftist government of President Manuel Azana. Early in the war, which began on July 17, 1936, the government, with minor backing of Russia, kept key cities like Madrid, Barcelona and Valencia while Franco's forces, backed by Germany and Italy with both men and munitions, began to move up from its southern stronghold to capture northern objectives and lay siege to government bastions.

After 10 days in the field observing both sides, Gibbons went to Madrid to broadcast to the States on station EAQ. Arriving at the studio he found a dozen loyalist soldiers, bayonets fixed, with orders to shoot if Gibbons uttered a word against the Spanish republic. None of the men spoke English.

President Franklin Roosevelt. After the Bonus March of 1932, Gibbons became disillusioned with Hoover and for the first time endorsed a presidential candidate, Franklin Roosevelt, for whom he made several campaign speeches. Gibbons met with him at least twice in the Oval Office, on March 26, 1934, over tea with Mrs. Roosevelt to discuss the economic recovery program, and March 11, 1936.

MARCH 26 86 *Mon*

APPOINTMENTS		APPOINTMENTS	
8.00		2.15	
8.15		2.30	
8.30		2.45	
8.45		3.00	
9.00		3.15	
9.15		3.30	
9.30		3.45	
9.45		4.00	
10.00		4.15	
10.15		4.30	
10.30		4.45	
10.45		5.00	
11.00	Mr. Dawes + Major Lohr	5.15	Floyd Gibbon (Tea)
11.15	Cong. Magnus Johnson + Abins	5.30	Messrs. Sloan, Chapin
11.30		5.45	+ Kelly
11.45	Cong. Sweeney + Dele	6.00	
12.00		6.15	
12.15	Cong. Abernethy	6.30	
12.30	Sec. Roper	6.45	
12.45	(Grenville Clark + Family)	7.00	
1.00	Amb. Dodd	7.15	
1.15	(Sloan, Kelly, Chapin)	7.30	
1.30		7.45	
1.45		8.00	
2.00		8.15	

Roosevelt appointment book for 1934.

First lady Eleanor Roosevelt met with Gibbons on May 1, 1934, at the White House to arrange for her appearance on Gibbons' new Johns-Manville-sponsored show called The American Home *on May 13. The appearance focused on the government's home construction programs. She liked the radio experience so much she began her own show, including music and her commentary.*

71

Wednesday

MARCH 11

APPOINTMENTS		APPOINTMENTS	
8.00		2.15	
8.15		2.30	
8.30		2.45	
8.45		3.00	
9.00		3.15	
9.15		3.30	
9.30		3.45	
9.45		4.00	
10.00		4.15	
10.15		4.30	
10.30		4.45	
10.45	*Sen. McAdoo*	5.00	
11.00	*Cong. Cullen & L.I. Delegation*	5.15	
11.15	*James G. Wolfe*	5.30	
11.30	*Judge Edwin L. Garvin*	5.45	
11.45	*Cong. Darden*	6.00	
12.00	*Frederick Osborn*	6.15	
12.15	*Rex Tugwell & Act. Dir. Bell*	6.30	
12.30	*Floyd Gibbons*	6.45	
12.45		7.00	
1.00	*Sen. Barkley*	7.15	
1.15		7.30	*Little Cabinet Dinner*
1.30		7.45	
1.45		8.00	
2.00	*Sumner Welles*	8.15	

Roosevelt appointment book for 1936.

Gibbons cleared his throat and signaled the station manager to turn on his microphone. He leaned in and declared that he had just "had to step across the bodies of twenty dead Spanish students lying out in the square." The English-speaking station manager killed the microphone. Listeners in the states were told there were technical difficulties. Gibbons persuaded him to relent and began again, but by now government censors fluent in English had arrived. As a result, during this and subsequent newscasts to the U.S. Gibbons had little of consequence to report.

"It is impossible for one who has not been there to believe the brutality of the war in Spain," he said later. "At one time, I saw eight hundred rebel soldiers lined up against a wall and executed without even the formality of a trial."

Toward the tail end of his month-long stay in Spain, Gibbons longed to get to France to broadcast freely of the massacres. The French, however, balked and he was limited to slipping into France at the southern French border town of Hendaye and traveling through Paris before embarking to New York on the *Normandie* on Sept. 23. Gibbons was combat-weary—the Spanish war had been his ninth conflict, more than any other reporter in the world, and he meant to curtail overseas work.

Barely off his ship, Gibbons took the train to Chicago and Kenosha, Wisconsin, to meet with executives of Nash Motors Company, who were sponsoring his weekly CBS broadcast of the Nash Motors *Speedshow*. The show, opening Oct. 3 in New York, would feature Gibbons as the master of ceremonies with his familiar staccato patter, accompanied by spirited Vincent Lopez and his orchestra.

Gibbons resumed his life of radio, movie and public speaking. He attended testimonial dinners, opening nights and fired the starter pistol for walkathons. He received the Italian War Cross for Military Valor in Ethiopia and a similar decoration from the Poles for his coverage of their conflict with the Russians.

But for the first time in his life he thought seriously of settling down. He purchased a 150-acre farm near Stroudsburg, Pa., and spent more and more time there between show business duties. He found he liked the life of the gentleman farmer, buying 3,000 chickens and, like his father before him, becoming an egg man, supplying local hotels and stores—though not driving the wagon himself. True to the old man's sales standard, he proposed selling autographed eggs and explored trademarking them as "vitamized." Gibbons wandered Cherry Valley Farm with a pair of Irish setters, hunting and shooting clay targets. His herds of sheep and pigs reproduced and an orchard and vegetable garden flourished. In a sentimental mood, he moved his parents' original 14th Street Washington, D.C., bed from his brother's house to his. At 52, Gibbons seemed to be settling into a comfortable life, even if the martial clatter coming from Europe did get his war correspondent juices flowing. He was on the farm on Sept. 1, 1939, to hear his decade-old warnings about Hitler borne out when the Nazis invaded Poland. Anticipating going to cover the war, he went to New York to make arrangements. The International News Service signed him up, and he cancelled the lease on his penthouse, put his yacht on the block and consulted his stockbrokers on investment strategy. But even this exertion proved too much. He was fatigued and short of breath. He returned to the farm accompanied by a nurse and a doctor.

Gibbons continued to monitor the war in Europe through the radio and newspapers, still envisioning yet another war to cover. The farmhouse walls acquired a layer of maps on which he tracked the battles of the day. But his health continued to decline and three weeks after the war began, Gibbons, in the bed he was born in, died of a heart attack on Sept. 24, 1939, at 10:15 p.m.

Fellow reporters, honoring the industry tradition of vying to see who could keen the most evocatively, mourned Gibbons like a dead king, hauling out endless variations on the vocabulary used to describe the result when ambition and talent collide with opportunity in a big-city newsroom: swashbuckling, adventurous, thrill-seeking, restless, trouble-hunting, roving and unorthodox. In time, the name "Floyd Gibbons" would come up in discussions of the fictional archaeologist Indiana Jones.

A *New York Times* obituary cast Gibbons as "the internationally known correspondent and radio commentator who seemed to have devoted his life to the search of thrills." He "differed from most publicized personalities in that he actually lived up to his publicity."

Japanese Admiral Kichisaburo Nomura being interviewed by Gibbons in Shanghai. Nomura later became the Japanese ambassador to the U.S. and through much of 1941 negotiated to prevent war between the two countries. He was in Washington on Dec. 7 when Japan attacked Pearl Harbor but always denied he had knowledge beforehand of the Japanese plan. (Corbis photo)

Nomura, Secretary of State Cordell Hull and Japanese Special Envoy Saburo Kurusu at their last meeting, in Washington, on Nov. 17, 1941.

By chance, Gibbons shared his final day on earth with eminent psychiatrist Sigmund Freud. *Cleveland Plain Dealer* columnist William McDermott, who had known Gibbons in Paris when he was *Tribune* bureau chief, wrote that the newsman and the mind healer, as different as chalk and cheese, nonetheless were symbols of their times.

Freud espoused "a theory of psychology which had a wide influence on literature and drama as well as on the treatment of mental maladjustments." Gibbons, he said, represented the "romantic type of American journalist, the adventurer [and] picturesque reporter." Freud, he wrote, "burrowed patiently under the appearances of things to find some underlying reality, while Gibbons "reported the surfaces of realities with great glibness and gusto."

McDermott wrote that Gibbons looked "the part of the war correspondent as the movies conceive the type…lean and erect, his not unhandsome face was made striking and unforgettable by the …patch that covered a sightless eye. Everybody knew he had suffered the injury in the line of service as a war correspondent, and it made him an arresting figure in any company."

McDermott posited that it might be for the best that Gibbons died while preparing to go cover another war. "It may be that the war of 1914-18 was the last great chance for journalism of the spectacular personal sort," he added, noting that the latest conflict's hordes of combat correspondents and squads of censors surely would have gotten Gibbons' goat. Though most fellow reporters hewed to the journalists' code of writing only good of a dead colleague, Gibbons had been, after all, a towering figure in his business whose time had passed, and he was fair game for criticism even on the undertaker's cooling board. In its obituary, *Variety,* called his rapid-fire delivery "passé."

Gibbons had said he wanted his ashes scattered by airplane above Paris, but his family wanted him buried with his parents. A funeral mass took place at Dahlgren Chapel of the Sacred Heart at Georgetown University in Washington, the hometown Gibbons had outgrown decades long ago but never quite left behind. Long after, writer James Bellah recalled a scene that stuck with him from that day. As relatives, colleagues, admirers, and curiosity-seekers prepared to follow the hearse to Mount Olivet Cemetery all the way across town, a man leaned into one of the vehicles queuing up for the cortege and asked to ride along. "He had been a postman in New York for years. One of the little men. But his moment had come once before," Bellah wrote in *Irregular Gentlemen*. Shot in a robbery, the letter carrier was out of work, with no possibilities. His sad saga came to Gibbons' attention. "Floyd had dug the incident out, furbished it, and presented it to the world," Bellah explained. Thanks to that coverage, the man got a job at the main post office as a special policeman "with very little to do in his frail, declining years but draw his salary and worship the name of Floyd Gibbons."

Bellah was graveside that rainy fall day, standing with a fellow writer as the coffin went into the red clay.

"That's the epitaph," the other fellow whispered. "Sacred to the memory of Floyd Gibbons, who knew one Honest Postman and Twenty Thousand Phonies."

Another friend and fellow deadline ace, Boake Carter, served as an honorary pallbearer. He remembered running into Gibbons not long before his death. A doctor had just told Gibbons how badly his heart had deteriorated. The physician recommended his patient stop smoking, stop drinking, and get more sleep. The news and accompanying recommendations had not gone down well with Gibbons.

Recounting the doctors' admonitions, Gibbons grew irate. "One eye flared in its blueness," wrote Carter. "He thumped his own chest over his heart and snorted in derision, '…and for what.'"

Scornful at the idea of moderation, Gibbons changed the subject to his upcoming assignment. "War! It was engulfing Europe again—the old stamping ground—the scenes of his original journalistic triumphs. Doctor or no doctor, heart or no heart, he wanted to go. He had to go. Anticipation throbbed within him. It was too much," Carter wrote. "His light burned brightly—then dimmed, then went out."

Floyd Gibbons' casket is carried from Dahlgren Chapel of Georgetown University following his death by heart attack on Sept. 23, 1939, as he prepared to cover the beginning of World War II. He left an estate of $255,000 ($4.2 million today) and divided it among his siblings and employees.

Gibbons family burial marker in Mt. Olivet Cemetery in Washington, D.C. Erected at the death of mother Emma in 1925, the Celtic cross marker, likely paid for by Floyd Gibbons, is far taller than the more modest markers nearby. It looks over an avenue named for St. Ignatius, founder of the Jesuit order that educated Floyd at Gonzaga and Georgetown. Gibbons' father Edward was buried there in 1934 after a funeral mass at Gonzaga's St. Aloysius Church. Brother Edward is also interred there. The eagle statuette at the neighboring gravestone bears an inscription that could have been written of Gibbons: "Eagles don't flock. They must be found one at a time."

FLOYD GIBBONS

ADVENTURER

Gibbons' clothing and typewriter at the Newseum in Washington, D.C. Gibbons wore a hat in the studio to protect his one eye from glare. Gibbons was well dressed and enjoyed fancy overcoats, including one entirely of animal fur that he wore on a trip to Japan and China with social commentator and pal Will Rogers. Rogers teasingly called the fur coat "flea-bitten and dogskin." Items are the Gift of The Family of Dorothy Gibbons Mitchell. (Photo Newseum/Courtesy Shelley Mitchell-Schaaf)

Notes

[1] Class of 1906. Through much of Gonzaga's history, substantial numbers of students beginning at Gonzaga did not graduate because of finances, moving or academics. Gonzaga's policy is to continue to affiliate these students with their class. Gibbons listed only Gonzaga and Georgetown for schooling in his listing for the 1922-23 *Who's Who in America*.

[2] Students studied DeHarbe's *Full Catechism*, focusing on faith and the Apostles' Creed and the Sacrament of Penance. In English class, Brown's *English Grammar* was the textbook of choice with emphasis on word etymology, penmanship, syntax, and letter-writing. Accompanying instruction in composition stressed analysis and parsing of sentences; to learn spelling and synonyms boys relied on Hazen's *Complete Speller*. Sadlier's *Excelsior U.S. History* carried students from the American Revolution to Grover Cleveland's second term. Mitchell's *New School Geography* explained the cultures and lands of North, South and Central America. *Latin Grammar* by Yenni declined nouns and adjectives, explained pronouns, explicated the active and passive voice of four regular conjugations, and illuminated fundamentals of syntax. Every other week boys had to compose a theme based on what they had learned in Latin grammar. In the second term they moved to Collar's *New Gradatim*, including a daily translation and parsing of stories. The second term introduced Greek in the form of Yenni's *Greek Grammar* textbook. Greek also taught regular declensions of nouns and adjectives and presentation of pronouns and verbs. Teachers used Greenleaf's *Complete Arithmetic* and the Bryant and Stratton book on bookkeeping. A Gonzaga boy was to spend three hours an evening on homework.

[3] Gonzaga's 1821 original building foundation still serves as the foundation of a building at 917 F St. NW built by John's brother after the old Gonzaga was demolished in 1871. A stone from that foundation is on a pedestal at Gonzaga and is called "The Spirit Stone."

[4] Edward Gibbons' biography of his brother, *Floyd Gibbons, Your Headline Hunter*, is a prime resource for this biography. The book was published in 1953 by Exposition Press, New York.

[5] Gibbons, trained to get correct names, oddly misidentified the man who helped save his life as Oscar Hartzell. Gibbons and Lieutenant Arthur E. Hartzell didn't meet up again after Gibbons' wounding until 1935 when Hartzell was in New York.

Bibliography

Allen, Stookie. *Men of Daring*. New York: Cupples & Leon Company, 1933.

Axelrod, Allen. *Miracle at Belleau Wood: The Birth of the Modern U.S. Marine Corps*. Guilford, Connecticut: The Lyons Press, 2007.

Camp, Dick. *The Devil Dogs at Belleau Wood: U.S. Marines in World War I*. Minneapolis: Zenith Press, 2008.

Crozier, Emmet. *American Reporters on the Western Front*. New York: Oxford University Press, 1959.

Curran, S.J., Robert Emmett. *The Bicentennial History of Georgetown University: From Academy to University, 1789-1889*. Volume I. Washington, D.C.: Georgetown University Press, 1993.

Douglas, Susan J. *Listening In: Radio and the American Imagination, from Amos 'n' Andy and Edward R. Murrow to Wolfman Jack and Howard Stern*. New York: Times Books, Random House, 1999.

Durkin, S.J., Joseph, Ed. *Swift Potomac's Lovely Daughter: Two Centuries at Georgetown through Students' Eyes*. Washington, D.C.: Georgetown University Press, 1990.

Ford, Hugh, Ed. *The Left Bank Revisited: Selections from the Paris Tribune, 1917-1934*. University Park, Pennsylvania: The Pennsylvania State University Press, 1972.

Freeman, Joseph. *An American Testament: A Narrative of Rebels and Romantics*. London: Victor Gollancz Ltd., 1938.

Gibbons, Floyd P. *How the Laconia Sank and The Militia Mobilization on the Mexican Border*. Chicago: Daughaday and Company Publishers, 1917.

-----. *And They Thought We Wouldn't Fight*. New York: George H. Doran Company, 1918.

-----. *The Red Knight of Germany: The Story of Baron von Richthofen, Germany's Great War Bird.* Garden City, New York: Garden City Publishing, 1927.

-----. *The Red Napoleon.* New York: Grosset & Dunlap Publishers, 1929.

Gilbert, Douglas. *Floyd Gibbons, Knight of the Air.* New York: Robert M. McBride & Company, 1930.

Gonzaga College Board of Trustees, *Gonzaga College, An Historical Sketch From Its Foundation in 1821 to the Solemn Celebration of its First Centenary in 1921,* Washington, D.C., 1922.

Gonzaga College Board of Trustees, *Sketch of Gonzaga College From Its Foundation in 1821 Till The Celebration Of The Diamond Jubilee in 1896,* 1897, Washington, D.C.

Hamilton, John Maxwell. *Journalism's Roving Eye: A History of American Foreign Reporting.* Baton Rouge: Louisiana State University Press, 2009.

Hirshorn, Stanley. *General Patton: A Soldier's Life,* New York: HarperCollins 2003.

Hohenberg, John. *Foreign Correspondence: The Great Reporters and Their Times.* New York: Columbia University Press, 1964.

Knightley, Phillip. *The First Casualty: The War Correspondent as Hero and Myth-Maker from the Crimea to Iraq.* Baltimore: The Johns Hopkins University Press, 1975.

Lewis, Jon E., Ed. *World War II, The Autobiography.* London: Constable & Robinson Ltd., 2009.

Minnert Associates. *Xavier: Reflections on 150 Years 1847-1997,* New York: The College of St. Francis Xavier, 1997.

Randall, David. *The Great Reporters.* London: Pluto Press, 2005.

Root, Jonathan. *Halliburton: The Magnificent Myth.* New York: Coward-McCann, Inc., 1965.

Root, Waverly. *The Paris Edition, 1927-1934.* San Francisco: North Point Press, 1989.

Rosholt, Malcolm. *The Battle of Cameron Dam.* Published by Malcolm Rosholt, 1974.

Seldes, George. *Tell the Truth and Run.* New York: Greenberg Publisher, 1953.

Shirer, William. *20th Century Journey: A Memoir of the Life and Times.* New York: Simon and Schuster, 1976.

Spencer, Jr., Samuel R. *Decision for War, 1917.* Peterborough, New Hampshire: William L. Bauhan Publishers, 1953.

Thomas, Lowell. *Good Evening Everybody: From Cripple Creek to Samarkand.* New York: Avon Books, 1976.

Thompson, Dorothy. *Let the Record Speak.* Boston: Houghton Mifflin Company, 1939.

Warren, Paul. *In the Web of History: Gonzaga College High School and the Lincoln Assassination.* Washington, D.C.: VELLUM/New Academia Publishing, 2009.

----. and Michael Dolan, editors. *Echo Ever Proudly: Gonzaga College High School in the Press, 1821-1899.* Washington, D.C.: The Gonzaga Alumni Board of Governors, 2005.

Weber, Ronald. *News of Paris: American Journalists in the City of Light Between the Wars.* Chicago: Ivan R. Dee, 2006.

Graduate Papers

Eastin, Leroy. *Floyd Phillips Gibbons: a Biographical and Bibliographical Study,* Master's paper, Florida State University, 1956.

Nelson, Andrew. *Floyd Gibbons, a Journalistic Force of Nature in Early 20th Century America,* Master's Thesis, University of Nebraska, 2011.

About the Author

Paul Warren is publisher of Warren Communications News in Washington, D.C., which publishes *Communications Daily* and *International Trade Today*, among other news publications. He is author of *In the Web of History: Gonzaga College and the Lincoln Assassination* and co-editor of *Echo Ever Proudly: Gonzaga College High School in the Press 1821-1899* and a 1968 graduate of Gonzaga. He holds a bachelor's degree from Le Moyne College, Syracuse, N.Y. and was a reporter for the *Rochester (N.Y.) Times-Union* and the *Hornell (N.Y.) Evening Tribune*. In addition, he has written for the *New York Daily News, Sporting News* and *TV Guide*.

The author's grandfather, Fred Yeomans, served in the Army during World War I but did not go overseas. Henry Lansing, the author's great uncle, was partially disabled by mustard gas while fighting for the Army in France.